CW00809573

THE HUMOROUS MAGISTRATE (ARBURY)

THE MALONE SOCIETY
REPRINTS, VOL. 177
2011 (2012)

PUBLISHED FOR THE MALONE SOCIETY
BY MANCHESTER UNIVERSITY PRESS

Oxford Road, Manchester M13 9NR, UK
and Room 400, 175 Fifth Avenue, New York, NY 10010, USA
www.manchesteruniversitypress.co.uk

Distributed exclusively in the USA by
Palgrave, 175 Fifth Avenue, New York,
NY 10010, USA

Distributed exclusively in Canada by
UBC Press, University of British Columbia, 2029 West Mall,
Vancouver, BC, Canada V6T 1Z2

British Library Cataloguing-in-Publication Data
A catalogue record for this book is available from the British Library

Library of Congress Cataloging-in-Publication Data applied for

ISBN 978-0-7190-8699-1

Typeset by New Leaf Design, Scarborough, North Yorkshire

Printed by Berforts Information Press Ltd, Oxford

This edition of *The Humorous Magistrate* was prepared by Margaret Jane Kidnie, and checked by N. W. Bawcutt.

This is the second of the Malone Society's projected series of editions based on the plays in Arbury MS A414. The Society is grateful to Lord Daventry for kindly agreeing to deposit Arbury MS A414 in the Warwickshire County Record Office for the duration of the editor's work, and for permission to reproduce the play. Thanks are also due to Warwickshire County Record Office for permission to reproduce images from the Newdigate family papers.

March 2011 N. W. Bawcutt

INTRODUCTION

Provenance

The Newdigate manuscript plays came to light in 1976 when investigations by Peter Beal into the Newdigate papers, using an early twentieth-century list of them, led to the discovery of shelves of otherwise unrecorded manuscripts at Arbury Hall, the seat of the Newdigate family in Nuneaton, Warwickshire. There are five plays in total. Four of them are bound together as part of a miscellany of thirty-one items (accession number MS A.414) that also contains poems and other pieces of writing in a variety of hands. A list of the miscellany's contents is appended below. One of these plays, *The twice-chang'd Friar. A comedie*, is furnished with a title-page; T. H. Howard-Hill has assigned to the others the titles of *Ghismonda and Guiscardo, The Humorous Magistrate*, and *The Emperor's Favourite*. The fifth play is included among the Newdigate papers housed at the Warwickshire County Record Office. Like *Ghismonda and Guiscardo*, it relates the first tale of the fourth day in Boccaccio's *Decameron*; evidently an early draft of *Ghismonda and Guiscardo*, it has been assigned the title *Glausamond and Fidelia*.[1] The manuscripts were microfilmed and catalogued by the Warwickshire County Record Office after Beal's discovery of them, leading to T. H. Howard-Hill's independent announcement of the plays in 1980/88.[2] This is the first edition of *The Humorous Magistrate* to be published.

In 2005, an anonymous, untitled, and undated manuscript play housed in the Special Collections of the University of Calgary was identified as another version of the Arbury Hall manuscript known as *The Humorous Magistrate*. The Osborne manuscript, described fully in the accompanying Malone Society edition, is far less worked over than the Arbury version of the play. I have discussed the hands and possible dating of these two manuscripts elsewhere, and will briefly summarise my findings here; readers are encouraged to compare, in particular, Plates 6 and 10 in this edition against Plates 4 and 6 in the Malone Society edition of the Osborne manuscript.[3]

[1] Warwickshire County Record Office, MS CR136/B.766. Howard-Hill provides for all five plays an account of provenance and hand, and a description of their action in 'Boccaccio, *Ghismonda*, and its Foul Papers, *Glausamond*', *Renaissance Papers* (1980), 19–28, and 'Another Warwickshire Playwright: John Newdigate of Arbury', *Renaissance Papers* (1988), 51–62. The existence of four plays bound together in 'a seventeenth-century MS. volume from a Warwickshire library' was first noted by an anonymous contributor to *The Gentleman's Magazine* ('"The twice chang'd friar. A comedie": (MS. temp. Charles I)', *The Gentleman's Magazine*, 300 (1906), 285–90.

[2] 'Boccaccio, *Ghismonda*, and its Foul Papers, *Glausamond*', and 'Another Warwickshire Playwright'. Although Beal drafted a letter to the *Times Literary Supplement* about the plays when he discovered them, the Newdigate family did not at that time want publicity or a flood of enquiries about them.

[3] Margaret Jane Kidnie, 'Near Neighbours: Another Early Seventeenth-Century Manuscript of *The Humorous Magistrate*', *English Manuscript Studies 1100–1700*, 13 (2007),

The hands found in the two copies of *The Humorous Magistrate* date to around the second quarter of the seventeenth century, and are similar in their use of a secretary script through which is scattered italic forms; perhaps most noticeably today, *h* in both manuscripts takes its modern shape, not displaying the secretary descender. They also share a predisposition to add a flourish, resembling a miniscule *u*, to the top right corners of secretary capitals *G*, *S*, and sometimes *F*, and both hands show a marked tendency to place a small dot in the centre of secretary capitals *O*, *B*, *W*, *P*, and *V*. Other traits, however, distinguish the two hands. Terminal *s* in the Arbury Hall manuscript is formed as a loop, the ends of which intersect to form a cross at the top of the letter; the Osborne manuscript, by contrast, prefers a form that looks like an *o* with a hook at the upper right corner; terminal *e* in the Osborne manuscript is also usually hooked. The Osborne hand tends to write the crossed majuscule secretary *I* using a single continuous pen stroke, whereas the Arbury scribe lifts the pen to form the letter with two separate strokes; majuscule *C* in Osborne, but not in Arbury, looks like an *O* crossed with a horizontal bar; the loop of the miniscule *d* in the Osborne manuscript shows an exaggerated lean to the left, where the same letter in the Arbury manuscript is smaller and more upright; and the final ascender of majuscule *W* flips to the left in the Arbury manuscript and to the right in the Osborne manuscript.

Although habits of spelling as a potential sign of authorship must be treated with caution since in this period one can find marked inconsistencies even within a single manuscript, there is an exclusive preference in the Osborne manuscript for 'Spruce' as the spelling of the name of the play's romantic lead (it appears forty-two times), as opposed to the Arbury manuscript's strong preference for 'Spruse' (this spelling is used forty-one times, with the other appearing just ten times). The Osborne scribe also avoids writing 'you' with a superscript *u*, a form strongly preferred by the Arbury scribe, and signals an elided *m* or *n* by suspending above the previous letter a shape resembling a large *c*, rather than the lightly hooked bar found in the Arbury manuscript.

The most heavily revised section is the opening scene of the play up to the entrance of Wild's man, Iony, at line 291 (ff. 105–107v; see Plates 2–7). These pages are exceptional in that one can discern, in addition to the sorts of deletions and interlinings found throughout the manuscript, a distinct layer of revision in a spidery hand using a grey-black ink. This hand, designated here Hand B, occasionally uses what looks like a secretary *h* (even in italic speech prefixes) and a hooked *e* and *s* in the terminal position, similar to the hooked forms typical of the Osborne manuscript. Both instances of *you* found in a two-line Hand B insertion at lines 103–4 (see Plate 3) also show the Osborne spelling preference (without superscript *u*).

187–211. On dating the five Arbury plays, also see Howard-Hill, 'Another Warwickshire Playwright'.

On the basis of what he describes as a 'diversity' of hand shared among the playscripts located in Warwickshire and personal papers comprised of three signed letters and a parliamentary diary, Howard-Hill has attributed the Arbury plays to John Newdigate III (1600–42).[4] Howard-Hill's conclusion is supported by the persuasive analyses of Boyda Johnstone and Kirsten Inglis, who document the distinctive features of the Arbury and Osborne hands recurring throughout Newdigate's writings in '"The Pen lookes to be canoniz'd": John Newdigate III, Author and Scribe.'[5] An extended discussion of Newdigate's hand can be found in the Malone Society introduction to the Osborne version of *The Humorous Magistrate*. It seems impossible entirely to discount the possibility that the particular and consistent patterns of handwriting one finds in the Osborne and Arbury Hall manuscripts of *The Humorous Magistrate* might belong to two writers whose habits were perhaps shaped by a common exemplar. However, the evidence for Newdigate as the plays' revising scribe—perhaps returning to the drama at different points in his career—is extremely strong. In this case, Hand B, while in some key respects dissimilar from the hand found elsewhere in the Arbury drama but sharing characteristics with the Osborne hand, probably also belongs to Newdigate. Passages attributed to Hand B are reproduced in bold font in this edition in order to signal this hand's appearance in the manuscript without cluttering the textual notes. If Newdigate did not write the playtexts during his possession of Arbury Hall in the 1620s and 1630s, it seems likely that he was somehow otherwise involved with their preparation, perhaps for instance through patronage or amateur performance—merely the provenance of the bulk of the manuscripts implies some kind of close connection during this period to the Newdigate estate.

Physical Characteristics of the Manuscript

The miscellany is contained within a plain binding of grey-blue card and half-leather measuring approximately 15.5 cm wide × 21.3 cm long (see Plate 1). There is a great disparity in the size of the bound leaves, ranging

[4] 'Another Warwickshire Playwright', p. 59. For the personal papers, see Warwickshire County Record Office, MS CR136/B.330, B.331, B.332, and MS CR136/A.1–3. This attribution has been in part accepted in the revised third edition of the *Annals of English Drama, 975–1700* (Alfred Harbage, rev. S. Schoenbaum, rev. Sylvia Stoler Wagonheim (London, 1989)). All five plays appear in the Anonymous Plays listings; the two plays that rework the story of Ghismonda (but not the other three), are cross-referenced to Newdigate in the Manuscript Author index. Vivienne Larminie, an authority on the sixteenth- and seventeenth-century Newdigate family, remains unconvinced by the attribution: 'Whilst John's interest in drama is undeniable, and his taste for writing poetry attested, whilst he was probably in the right place at the appropriate period, and whilst the hand in which the plays are written could easily be one of the several variations he adopted, the attribution of the plays seems to this writer to remain unproven' (*Wealth, Kinship and Culture: The Seventeenth-Century Newdigates of Arbury and Their World* (Woodbridge, Suffolk, 1995), p. 160, fn. 20).

[5] Kirsten Inglis and Boyda Johnstone, '"The Pen lookes to be canoniz'd": John Newdigate III, Author and Scribe', *Early Theatre*, 14:2 (2011), 27–61.

from about 19.5 cm wide × 18.3 cm long ('A proiect for A newe dignitie') to 15.5 cm wide × 22.6 cm long (verses beginning 'The freeborne English generous and wise'). These two one-page documents have been folded at the side and bottom, respectively. The four plays in the volume measure approximately 15.2 cm wide × 20.2 cm long (*Ghismonda*), 15.1 cm × 20.4 cm (*Humorous Magistrate*), 14.5 cm × 18.3 cm (*The Emperor's Favourite*), and 14.4 cm × 20.2 cm (*The Twice Chang'd Friar*).

The binding seems amateurish: the leather has been glued directly onto the textblock not allowing for a hollow, there are no headbands top or bottom, and the leather is finished within, rather than on top of, the paper covers. There are six raised bands on the spine, with 'MSS.MISCI' printed in a single row in badly flaking letters. The pastedown and uncut endpapers found at the front were made by folding a single sheet of paper in quarto (one of the quadrants, visible under the pastedown and beside the gutter, has been partially cut away to form a tab that was glued with the pastedown to the cover). The same process was repeated for the pastedown and uncut endpapers at the back. A shelfmark on the front pastedown reads 'S27'. On the recto of the volume's front endpapers is written a note which perhaps mentions the date at which the volume was bound: '1782 | Manuscript Plays | of considerable | interest | EO [Edgar Osborne] | A. 414'.[6] The cataloguing archivist, reading '1782' as '6782' (and so as a second shelfmark), suggests in a note attached to a separate contents page that '[t]he volume was probably made up in the early eighteenth century'. Dates on items elsewhere in the miscellany indicate that it must have been gathered and bound no earlier than 1702.

Excluding the modern endpapers, the miscellany consists of 229 leaves. They are numbered in pencil to folio 196 (actually 195 due to an error of numbering after 194) by the Warwickshire County Record Office archivist. The pencil numbering ends after the first leaf of *The Twice Chang'd Friar*, the final item in the volume. The leaves of *The Humorous Magistrate* (ff. 104–43) are also separately numbered in ink from 1–38 in the same hand that wrote out the text, beginning after the page on which is written 'The Names of the Actors' and the prologue. The original numbering is accurate, despite no number appearing on either leaf 37 or the terminal leaf on which is written the epilogue (leaf 39). Apart from the first unnumbered leaf (blank on the recto), and the last leaf containing the epilogue (blank on the verso), each leaf bears text on both sides. Discussion of the miscellany in this introduction follows the modern numbering and editorial line references.

The Humorous Magistrate includes at f. 139 a watermark with a pot design on which is worked the letters 'R H', standing upright and parallel to the gutter. This same watermark appears in eight other places, ranged across the gutter of the book (ff. 109–10, 113–14, 115–16, 119–20, 125–6, 127–8, 133–4, and 137–8). A second watermark figure of two pillars rising to a bunch of

[6] For Edgar Osborne's involvement with the Newdigate collection, see the Malone Society introduction to the Osborne version of *The Humorous Magistrate*.

grapes appears on the epilogue page and the blank that follows (ff. 143–4). The centre of the watermark is lost in the gutter, but the design otherwise closely resembles Heawood's figure 3492 (reproduced from a Lancastrian manuscript dated 1640).[7] This anomalous watermark may indicate that the epilogue was a late addition to the manuscript. This same pillars-and-grapes watermark reappears in the miscellany at f. 70, on which is written a one-page poem dated 'Aug. 1637' and entitled 'To a Poet whose m^ris^ was painted'. This poem exhibits the same distinctive scribal characteristics one finds in the Osborne manuscript. In 'Near Neighbours: Another Early Seventeenth-Century Manuscript of *The Humorous Magistrate*', I argue that if one assumes that the Arbury epilogue was a late addition to the manuscript, and that the writer of 'To a Poet' likely dated the poem to the month and year it was copied out (rather than to a possible earlier date of composition), the combination of hands and watermarks found in the Arbury miscellany and Osborne copy serves to establish an outer limit for the composition of *The Humorous Magistrate* to near or shortly after 1637.[8]

The Arbury version is written in an ink that varies from light to dark brown, and it has been heavily worked over. Words, phrases, lines, and whole speeches are deleted and often replaced with densely interlined new material, for the most part in what appear to be the same ink and hand (with one exception, discussed in the next paragraph). The author typically strikes out a passage with a single horizontal line, although occasionally one finds individual words and letters either blotted, smudged, hatched, or scribbled out and whole speeches cancelled with a set of vertical and/or diagonal lines. A long vertical penstroke appears in ink in the margin between the speech prefixes and body of the text at f. 126v, but it is not clear that this line serves to mark this extended stretch of dialogue for deletion.

There is also at least one revised false start. The writer initially brought the penultimate scene to a close with the entrance of the servant, Godfry, to announce the arrival of new guests; this ending is crossed out in order to continue the action with a long set piece in which a group of characters tries to decide the thing that angers a woman most. The scene in this modified form finally concludes with the introduction of a slightly revised version of Godfry's earlier entrance (ff. 139–139v). Thus the manuscript, at least in part, shows an author in the process of composition, an inference supported elsewhere in the document by a boxed note (written in the spidery hand and black ink of Hand B) that instructs that the play is 'Hitherto corected in this|⟨b⟩ooke from this place|in the other' (106v, lines 193–5; see Plate 5). On the reverse of the same page an italic note in the left margin running

7 Edward Heawood, *Watermarks: Mainly of the 17th and 18th Centuries* (Hilversum, Holland, 1950).

8 Martin Wiggins comments that the substitution of *Diar* (i.e. James Dyer) for *Cooke* in a joke about literary and legal works at 1177–9 might suggest that the play was written before Edward Coke's death in 1634; he dates its composition to the first half of 1634. See Martin Wiggins, *British Drama, 1533–1642: A Catalogue* (Oxford, 2012–).

vertically alongside the dialogue reads, 'Dr S. this speech not so cleare & ꝯspicuous' (see Plate 4). This note, seeming to invite response from a reader, reinforces the likelihood that this is a draft version. Howard-Hill speculates that this comment is addressed to John III's life-long friend and correspondent, Gilbert Sheldon (future Archbishop of Canterbury), who graduated from Oxford Doctor of Divinity in 1634.[9]

However, alongside such evidence of original composition in the Arbury manuscript, one also finds copying errors. The phrase 'take her away' near the end of the third act, for example, is wrongly given to Iennet, the housekeeper, who is pleading with her employer for mercy; this misassigned command is crossed out and written out again on the next line as the opening words of Thrifty's concluding speech (f. 124, lines 1670–1). At folio 125 (lines 1781–4), an overlooked short speech inserted into a revised sequence of dialogue between Godfry and Mistress Mumble led to two misassigned speech prefixes. The error was corrected by using the space deep in the gutter of the page to reverse the speech prefixes from '*mum*' to '*God*' and '*Godf:*' to '*Mum*'. The Arbury manuscript thus seems to offer an intermediate, but complete, draft of a play in progress, with the revising author functioning as his or her own copyist.[10]

The Present Text

The manuscript contains a large number of revisions that are introduced in the place of deleted words, phrases, and sometimes even whole lines. Such revision was fitted in as space would allow, frequently with the use of a caret to signal its intended place of insertion. Occasionally there was room on a line to position the revision directly following the deletion. In such cases, it is difficult to distinguish a specific act of revision with *currente calamo* alterations, but occasionally the colour of ink or changes in script that might result from a new quill allow one to discern a distinct stage of revision. More typically, revisions were squeezed in above and very occasionally below a cancelled passage. Cancelled words and lines are usually crossed out with a single line, marked in this edition with [square brackets]. Other forms of cancellation such as hatching, scribbling, smudging, and blotting are enclosed within square brackets (and also ⟨diamond brackets⟩ if the reading is illegible). Where a whole speech is cancelled using a set of vertical and diagonal lines, the cancellation is put in square brackets (double square brackets where individual lines are also crossed out), and the form the cancellation takes is noted in the collation.

[9] Howard-Hill, 'Another Warwickshire Playwright', 60.

[10] For further discussion of composition and revision practices in the drama preserved in the Arbury miscellany, see Siobhan Keenan's excellent discussion of 'Authorial Corrections' in the introduction to her Malone Society edition of *The Emperor's Favourite* (Manchester, 2011), pp. xiii–xxi.

All interlineations are signalled in this edition with ⌜corner brackets⌝, and where possible they are brought down into the body of the line. Where an interlineation is too long to fit into an existing line it appears on a separate line above or below the deleted passage it is meant to replace, positioned as closely as possible to its placement in the manuscript. Where revisions effected by Hand B are interlined (and in this edition either left interlined or brought down into the text line), they are in corner brackets like any other interlineation. No effort has been made to reproduce the tightly condensed lines and often smaller lettering typical of interlined revision, and complex or potentially confusing stages of revision are explained in the collation. Carets used in the manuscript to position an insertion are included in this edition; where the precise position of a caret cannot be reproduced, its location is noted in the collation (e.g. line 1325 *of* ^] caret positioned under *o*).

In some places the author has effected a revision by writing one or more letters over existing text. This edition reproduces the revised reading, and notes in the collation which letters are over others. The revising author also commonly squeezes letters into a gap between words. This tighter spacing is sometimes reproduced in the edition (e.g. *pressingme* at line 45; see Plate 2); whether or not the spacing is reproduced, a note in the collation explains the nature of the adjustment ('*ing* squeezed in'). Where a revision is written directly over the original text, the unrevised reading is given in the collation (e.g. *Exeunt.* at line 126, see Plate 3, where the collation note reads '*eunt.* over *it*').

There is no evidence that the pages were folded to provide separate columns for speech prefixes, dialogue, and marginal stage directions. The speech prefixes, however, seem to have been added after the dialogue was written out since they are sometimes cramped into the available space; only in one instance (line 3416) is the dialogue slightly indented to accommodate an overly long speech prefix. The space between speech prefixes and dialogue has been regularized, as have the spaces between letters and between words. The relative position of stage directions and the five act breaks to the dialogue is reproduced as closely as print will allow, as is the placement of tildes (in this manuscript always a lightly hooked bar). The boxes and partial boxes commonly used to set off stage directions are reproduced in this edition. The exact placement of superscript letters has not been replicated (the *u* of 'yo^{u}' and *r* of 'yor' sometimes appear directly above rather than to the right of the *o*); however, at 551, 783, and 937 this edition records where a superscript letter is positioned in a medial rather than terminal position (e.g. 'y^{u}o') due to space restrictions. Instances of punctuation positioned under superscript letters have been regularized to follow the superscript letter. An eccentricity of the scribe's hand, found only on ff. 130r–132v, is the recurrent, but not invariable, formation of italic *in* as a dotted flat, or nearly flat, line. This irregularity occurs with *King* used as a speech prefix and in one stage direction, and once in the dialogue with the word *fekins* (see Plate 10). It is difficult to do justice in print to this feature of the manuscript since a straight line (i.e. *K—g* and *fek—s*) not only omits the dot, but might suggest deliberately omitted letters, rather than instances of what is for this hand unusually shaped letter forms. This quirk, which appears twenty-seven times in the manuscript, is not reproduced in the edited text, the words in question reading in these places either *King* or *fekins*.[11]

Italic is typically used for speech prefixes, stage directions, and Latin words and phrases, and it is also occasionally used in the dialogue for names and professions (e.g. *Clerk* at 65 and *Cupids* at 228). Some instances of italic are difficult to discern with certainty, the difference between mixed secretary and italic words often depending on letter spacing (the letters of italicized words tend to be more deliberately spaced), habits of usage at that point in the manuscript, and especially the form of certain distinctive letters such as *c*, *e*, *r*, *s*, *G*, *I*, and sometimes *g* and *y*. Uncertain instances are noted in the collation. In a similar manner, some majuscules in this mixed hand are difficult to distinguish from their miniscule forms: *C*, *D*, *F*, *M*, *W*, and *Y*—particularly with regard to the speech prefixes for Mumble and Wild—are consistently problematic. Frequently these letters, in shape and/or size, seem to fall somewhere between the majuscule and miniscule forms. Where it is unclear which is intended, a decision has been made based on context and the tendencies of usage at that point in the manuscript.

I would like to thank Martin Wiggins for introducing me to the Arbury plays back in 1991. I am indebted to Mark Booth at the Warwickshire County Record Office for liaising on my behalf with Lord Daventry about the miscellany and for sharing with me his knowledge of the Newdigate collection. I am further grateful to Robert Pitt for preparing the images and sharing with me his knowledge of bindings, and to Siobhan Keenan and Lesley Caine for kindly double-checking some final readings in the manuscript before the edition went to press. Sean Henry provided invaluable assistance reformatting the first draft of the edition to conform to Malone Society conventions. The research for this edition was undertaken with the aid of a travel grant and sabbatical leave from the University of Western Ontario in 2005, and a Collaborative Research Grant from the Social Sciences and Humanities Research Council of Canada, 2006–9. Finally, James and Will Purkis accompanied me to Warwick for two weeks in December 2008 when Will was just five months old, making possible the timely completion of this research. This edition is dedicated to James and Will.

[11] The irregularity appears in the speech prefixes at lines 2239, 2243, 2251, 2253, 2260, 2265, 2277, 2289, 2291, 2294, 2300, 2312, 2317, 2320, 2322, 2325, 2328, 2383, 2410, 2412, 2424, 2436, 2449, 2453, and 2462, it appears in the stage direction at 2457, and italic *fekins* is found at 2439.

Appendix: Miscellany Contents (MS A.414)

f. 1 'The Style of Henry the Second Prince of Grayes Inne Anno Dm. 1617'

f. 13 'To the Kings most excellent ma^{tie}'

ff. 15–16 uncut blanks

f. 17 'A Character of an Anabaptist By Mr Geary of Barrwell'

f. 24 'A proiect for A newe dignitie; betweene Barrons and knights'

f. 25 'The heads of ye 14 Articells exhibited agst the Chancellor 10th July: 63 ꝑ Earle of Bristoll'

f. 26 'Aduertisem^{ts} vpon the present estates of Germanie and Bohemia Ano 1620' to which is appended in another hand the following note: 'Perswading the french King rather to aid Frederick then Ferdinand. It seemes to bee written by a french man no freind to the house of Austria'

f. 36 'In restitutam Hungariæ Libertatem; et fælicem Illustrissimi Principis Iosephi Inaugurationem'

f. 38 'Exercitationes Poeticæ habitæ Etonæ Velatarum Ad Nativitatem Christi 1702' by John Parker, John and Joseph Neale, J. Ludford, Richard Holme, W. Liptrott, John Foxcroft, and Samuel Balie.

f. 50 'Second Advice to a Painter' (title attributed by archivist)

f. 56 'Advice to a Painter. A Lampoon' (title attributed by archivist)

f. 58 'Mr. William Cartwright on the successes of November' (title attributed by archivist)

f. 60 'Vers envoyes de Paris sur l'entrée de My Lord Portland'

ff. 61–2 Two untitled poems

f. 63 'A New Littany for the Holy time of Lent. 1688'

f. 64 'Addition to the Old mans wish "if I live to grow Old etc"'

f. 65 'Mr Brownes ꝉre to his sweet harts mother. Fellow of Trin. Col. in Ox: 1618'

f. 66 Verses beginning 'The freeborne English generous and wise'

f. 67 'In the praise of Folly' beginning 'Happy the man whose friendly want of wit | makes him for all things | but contempt unfit'; on 68v is written in another hand what seems to be an abandoned draft letter 'To ye Lady Iane Smyth'

f. 69 'A song at the Election in Coventry' (title attributed by archivist)

f. 70 'To a Poet whose m^{ris} was painted.' The original title 'Vpon a painted gentlewoman.' is struck out. It is dated Aug. 1637.

f. 71 Verses entitled 'Dr. Corbet To ye duke of Buckingham.'

f. 73 'A Dream of Elisium'. Verses signed Newdigate.

f. 75 'The Satyrs Complaint.'

f. 77 *Ghismonda* (title attributed by T. H. Howard-Hill)

f. 103 Page that is blank on verso and on recto reads 'Plays' in top right corner

f. 104 *The Humorous Magistrate* (title attributed by T. H. Howard-Hill)

f. 144	blank
f. 145	*The Emperor's Favourite* (title attributed by T. H. Howard-Hill)
f. 195	ghost folio—archivist's numbering skips from 194 to 196
f. 196	'The twice chang'd friar. A comedie.'

The pages in the Plates have been reproduced at approximately 82 per cent of full size.

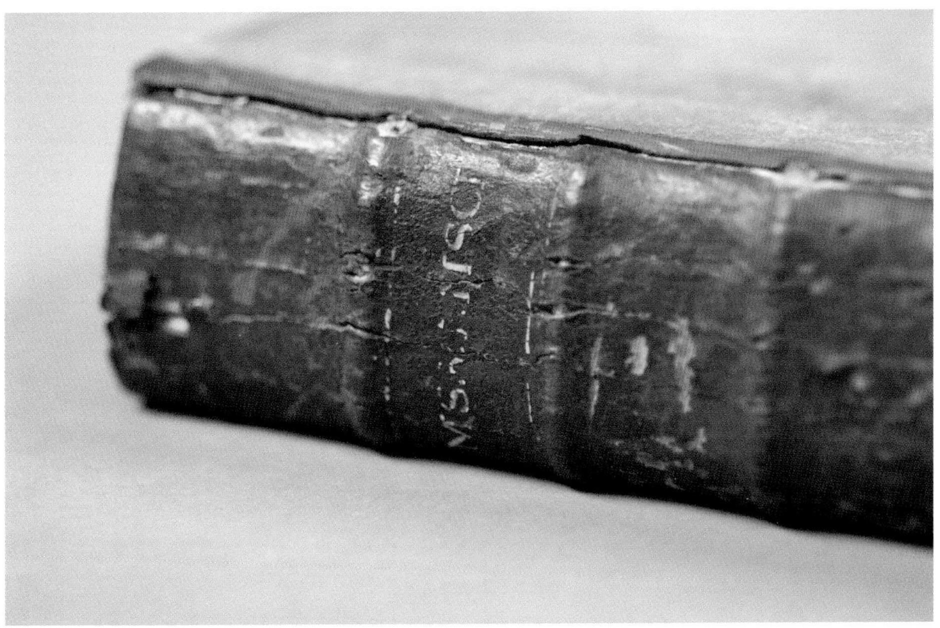

PLATE 1: THE ARBURY MISCELLANY (MS A.414).
Reproduced with permission of Lord Daventry

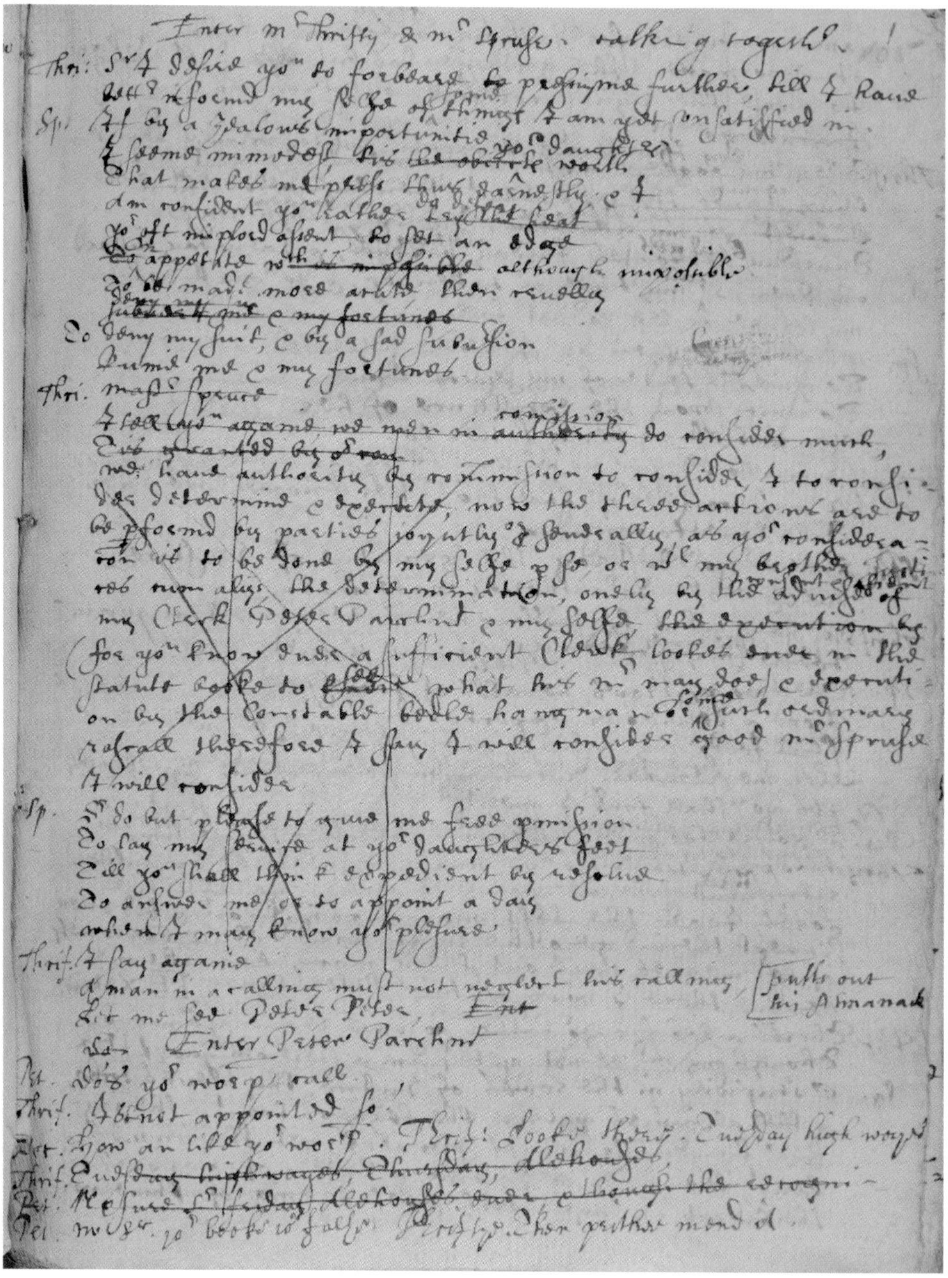

PLATE 2: *THE HUMOROUS MAGISTRATE*, ARBURY MANUSCRIPT (MS A.414), 105r. Reproduced with permission of Lord Daventry

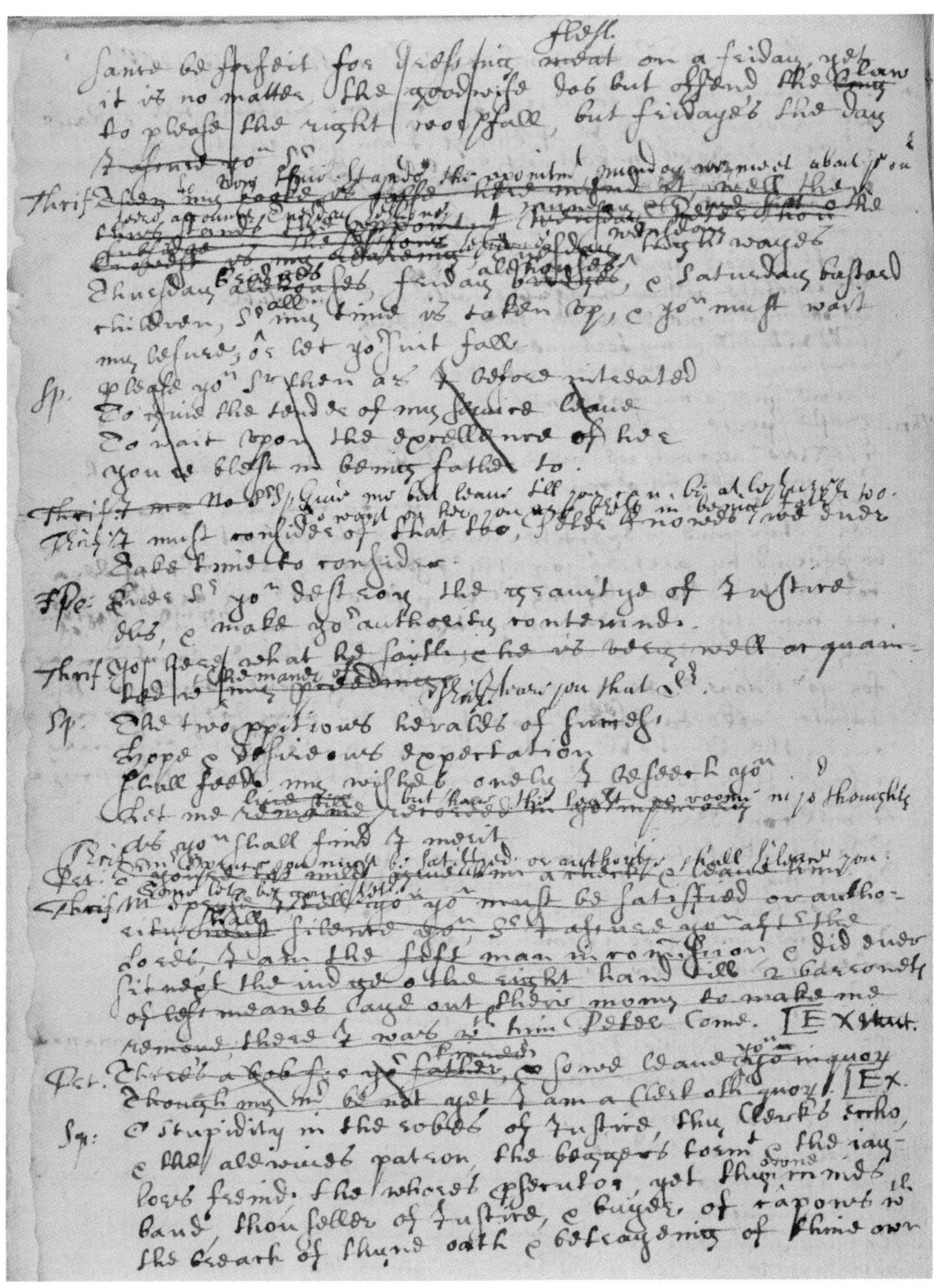

PLATE 3: *THE HUMOROUS MAGISTRATE*, ARBURY MANUSCRIPT (MS A.414), 105v. Reproduced with permission of Lord Daventry

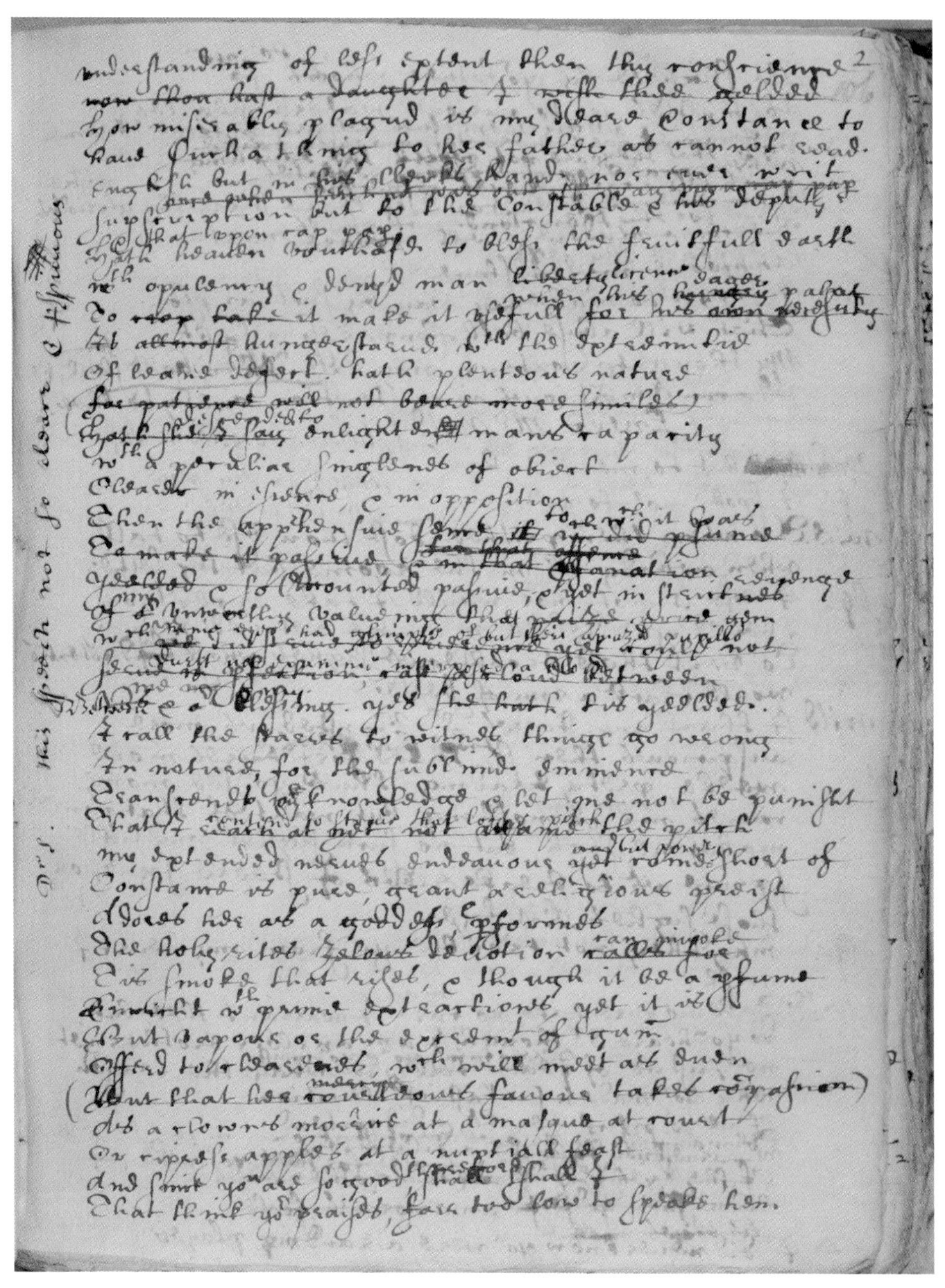

PLATE 4: *THE HUMOROUS MAGISTRATE*, ARBURY MANUSCRIPT (MS A.414), 106r. Reproduced with permission of Lord Daventry

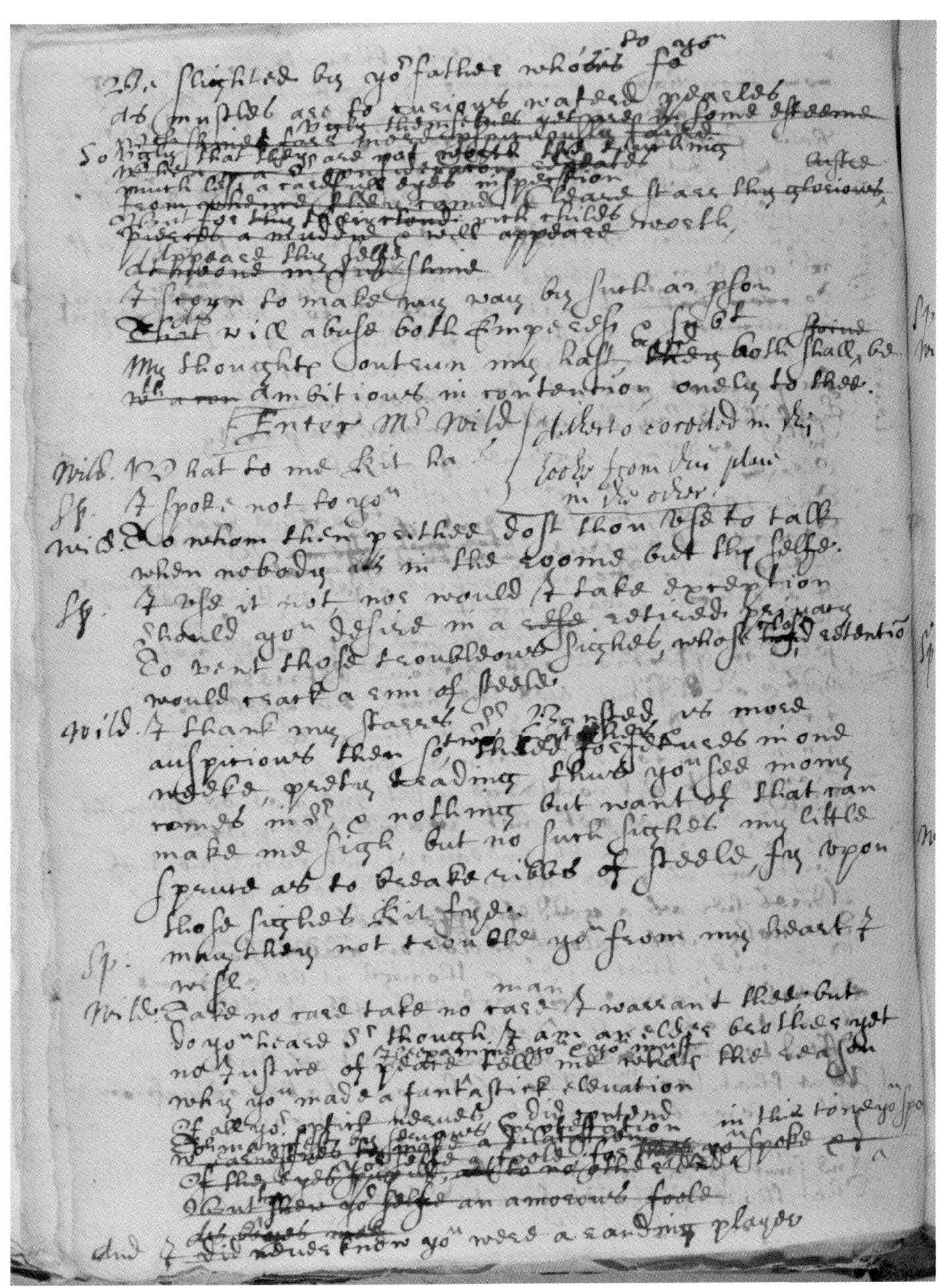

PLATE 5: *THE HUMOROUS MAGISTRATE*, ARBURY MANUSCRIPT (MS A.414), 106v. Reproduced with permission of Lord Daventry

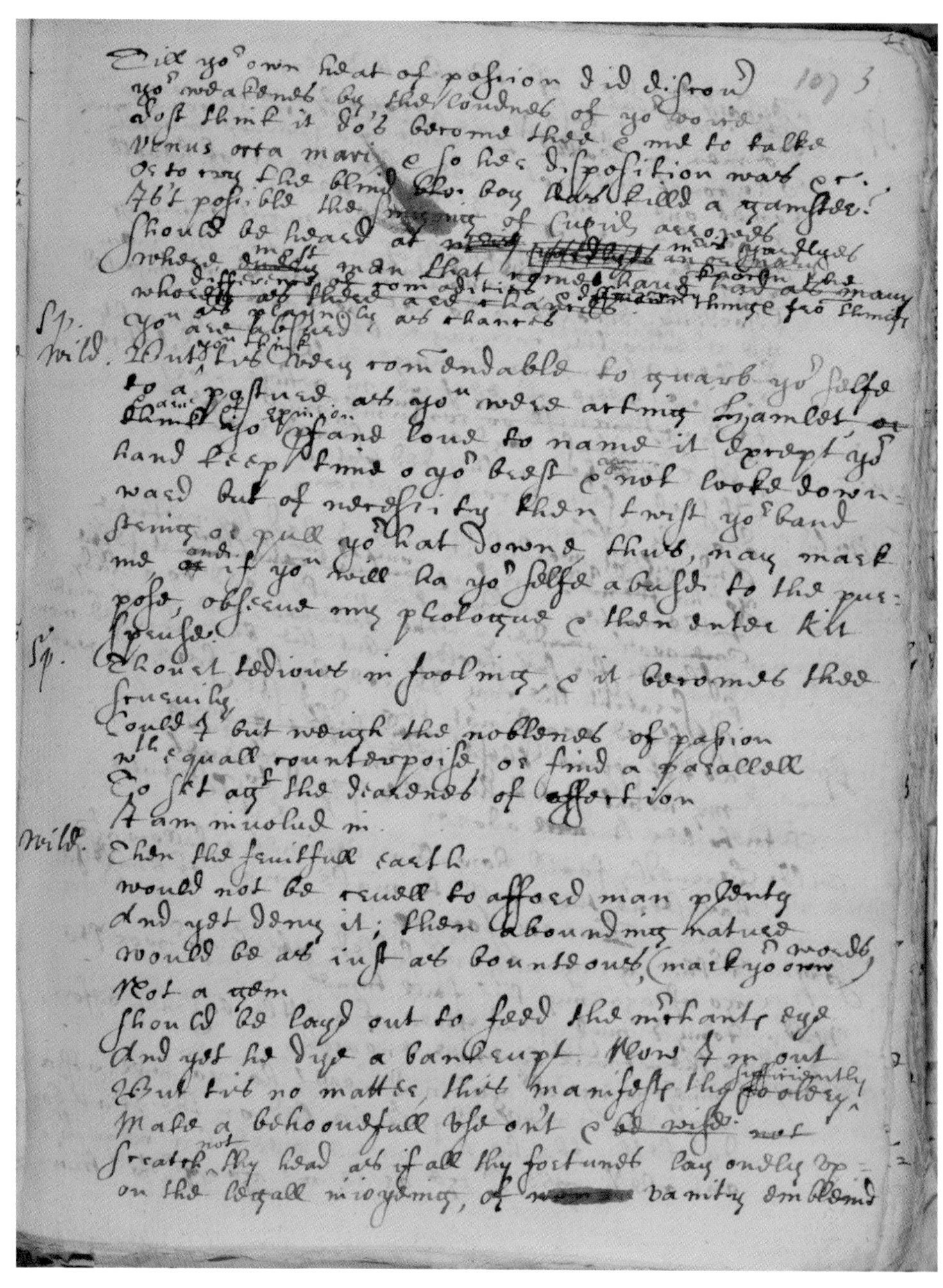

PLATE 6: *THE HUMOROUS MAGISTRATE*, ARBURY MANUSCRIPT (MS A.414), 107r. Reproduced with permission of Lord Daventry

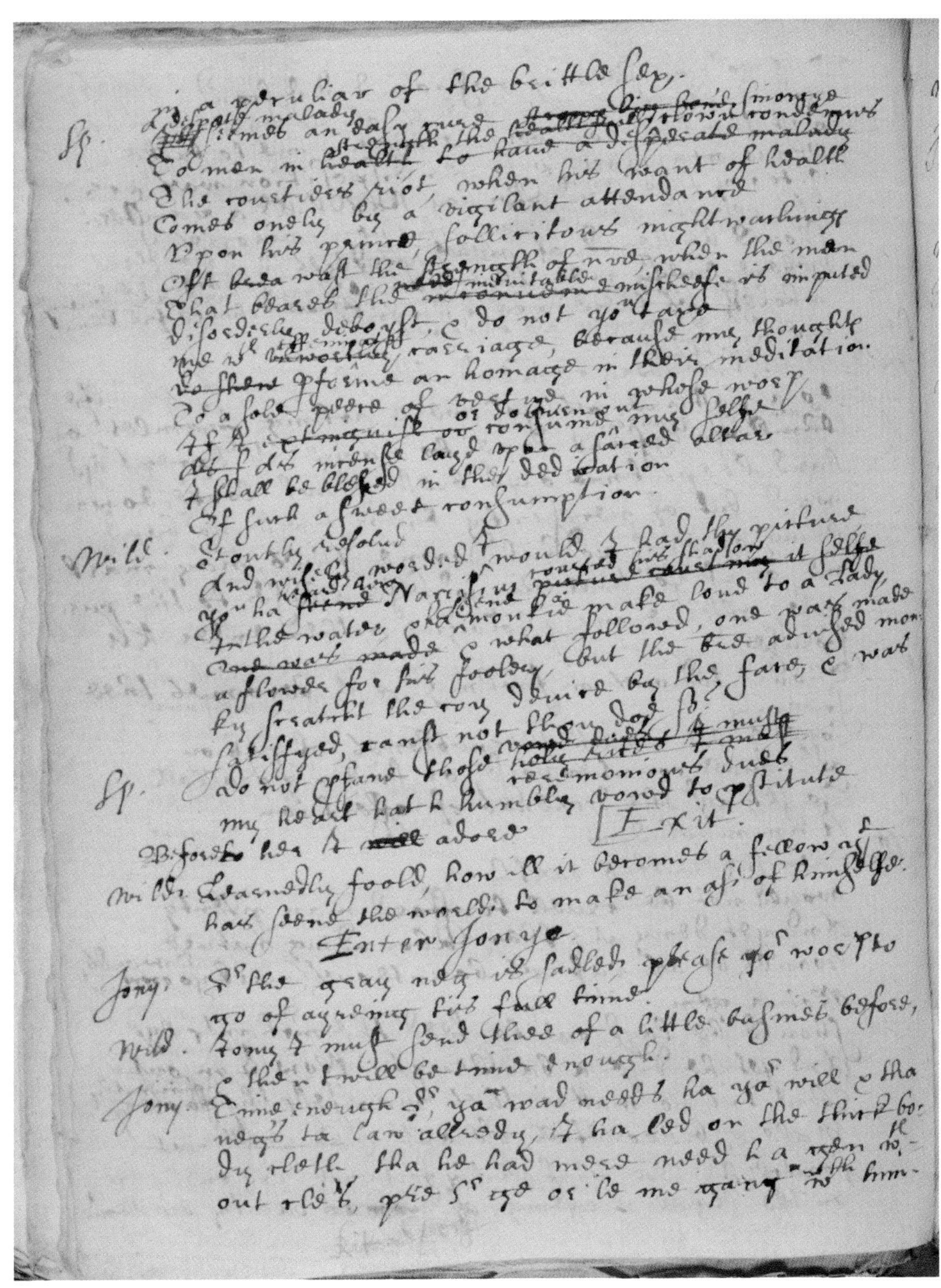

PLATE 7: *THE HUMOROUS MAGISTRATE*, ARBURY MANUSCRIPT (MS A.414), 107V. Reproduced with permission of Lord Daventry

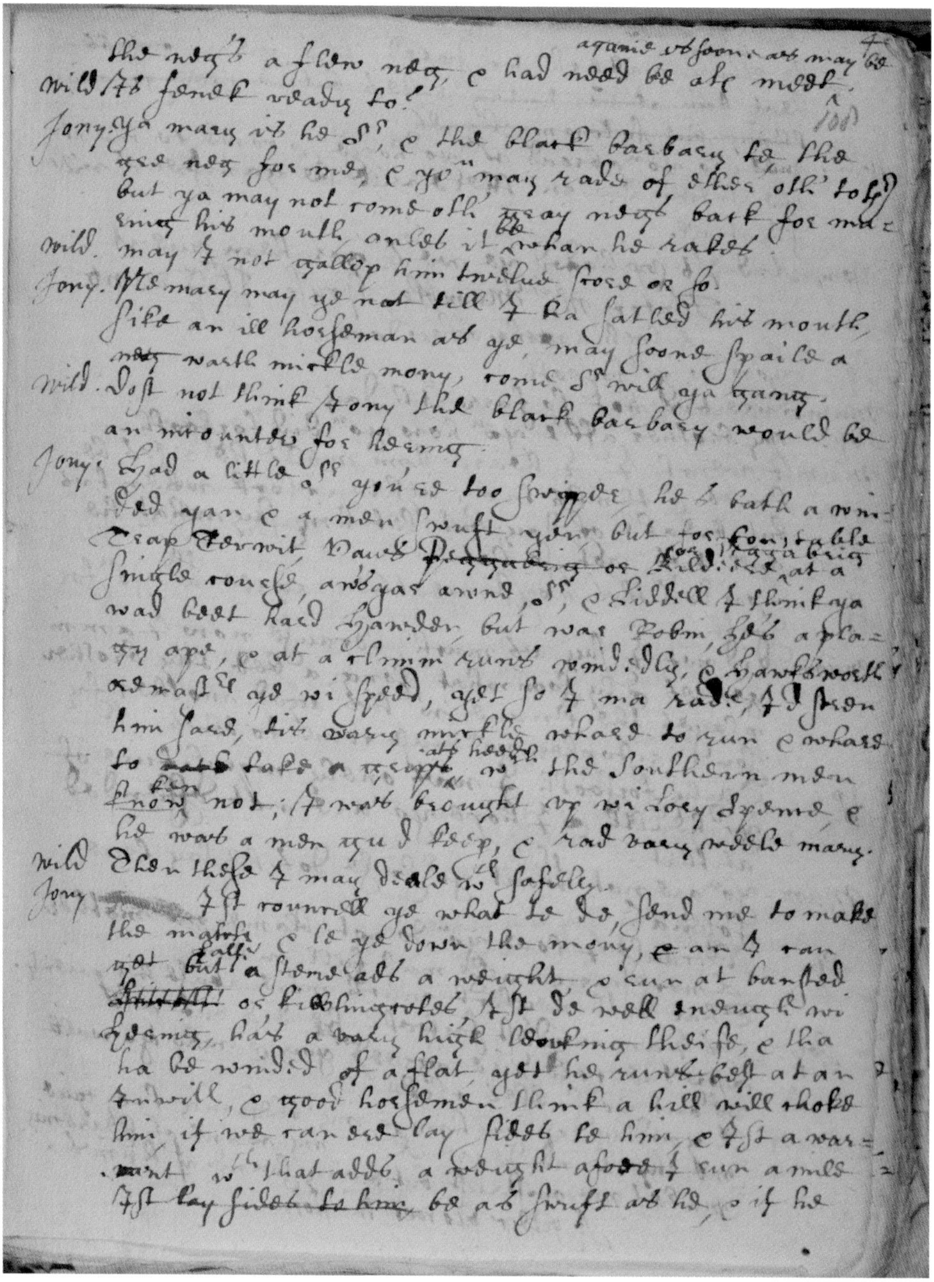

PLATE 8: *THE HUMOROUS MAGISTRATE*, ARBURY MANUSCRIPT (MS A.414), 108r. Reproduced with permission of Lord Daventry

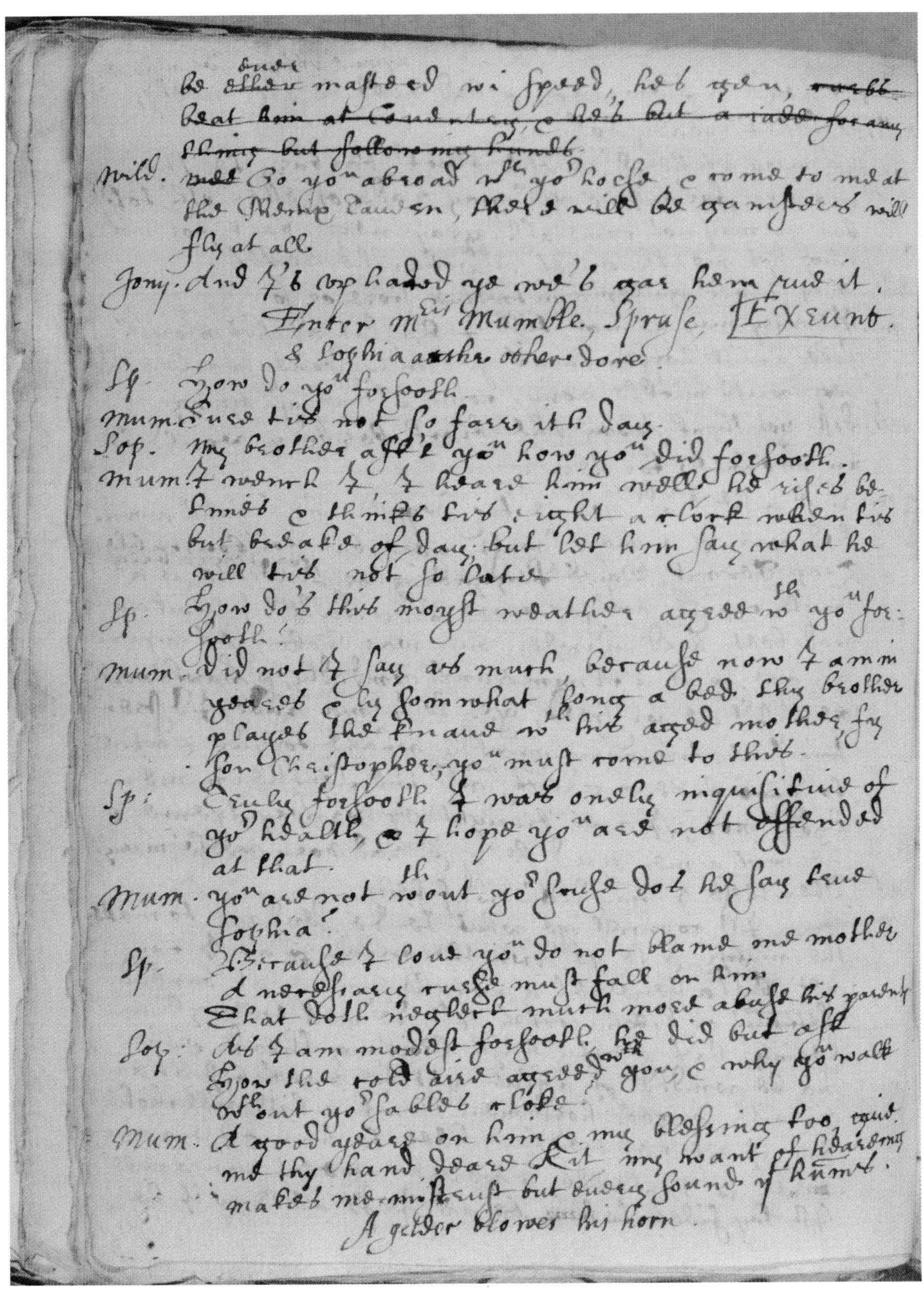

Wild. Go you abroad wth yo[r] hoss & come to meet the Merry Dawson, there will be gamsters will fly at all

Jony. And if's orphaned ye we's gar hem rue it.

Enter M[rs] Mumble. Spruse, & Sophia at the other dore. Exeunt.

Sp. How do you forsooth.

Mum. Sure tis not so fare ith day.

Sop. My brother ask't you how you did forsooth.

Mum. I warrant I heare him well he rises betimes & thinks tis right a clock when tis but breake of day; but let him say what he will tis not so late.

Sp. How do's this moyst weather agree wth you forsooth?

Mum. Did not I say as much, because now I am in yeares & ly somwhat long a bed thy brother playes the knave w[th] his aged mother, fy son Christopher, you must come to this.

Sp. Truly forsooth I was onely inquisitive of yo[r] health, & I hope you are not offended at that.

Mum. You are not w[th]out yo[r] sauce doth he say true Sophia?

Sp. Because I love you do not blame me mother
A necessary rush must fall on him
That doth neglect much more abuse his parents

Sop. As I am modest forsooth, he did but ask how the cold aire agreed w[th] you, & why you walk w[th]out yo[r] sables cloke.

Mum. A good yeare on him & my blessing too, give me thy hand deare Kit my want of hearing makes me mistrust but every sound of humes.

A gelder blowes his horn.

PLATE 9: *THE HUMOROUS MAGISTRATE*, ARBURY MANUSCRIPT (MS A.414), 108v. Reproduced with permission of Lord Daventry

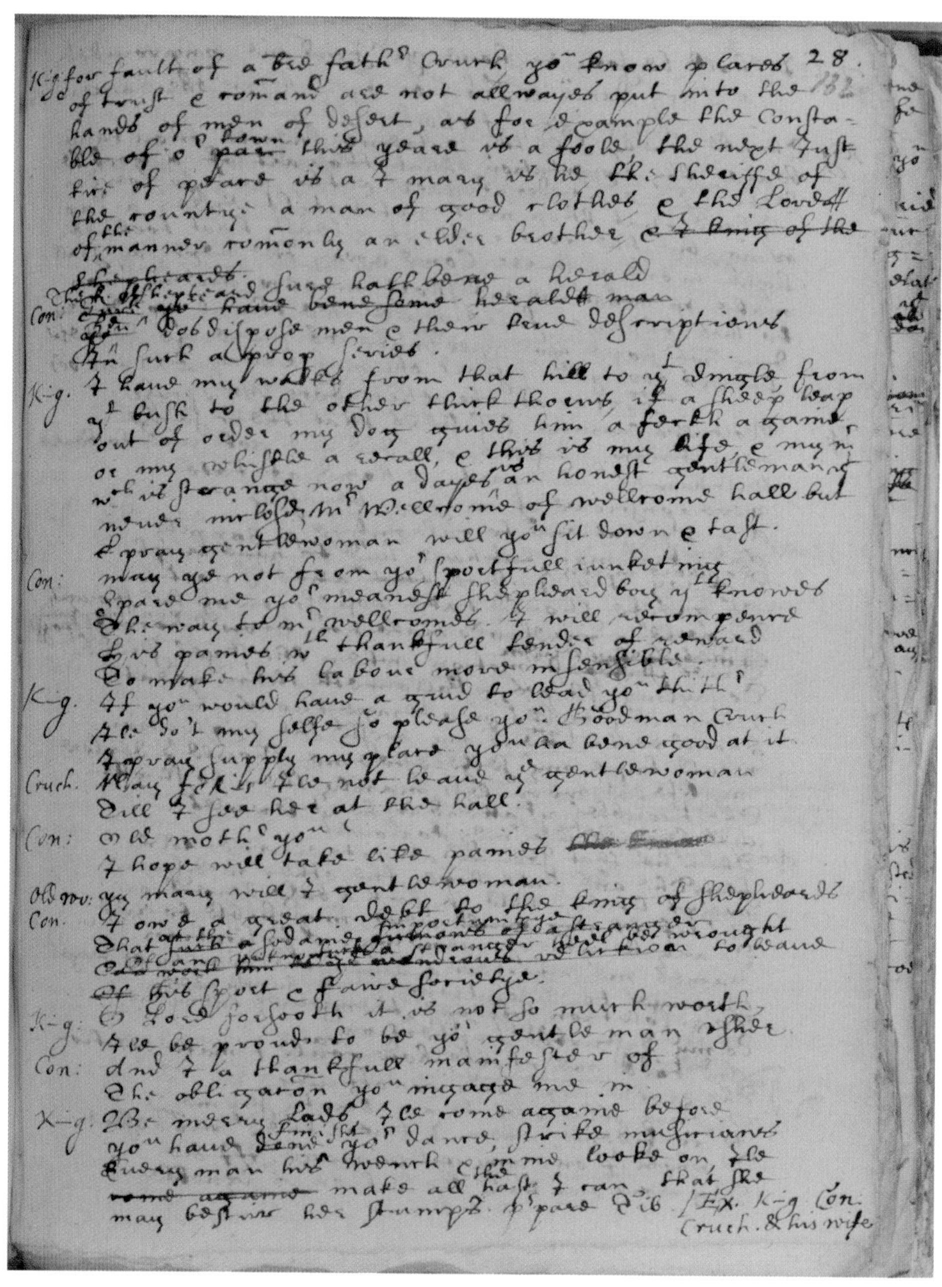

PLATE 10: *THE HUMOROUS MAGISTRATE*, ARBURY MANUSCRIPT (MS A.414), 132r. Reproduced with permission of Lord Daventry

[FOL. 104v]

The Names of the Actors.

Mr Thrifty a Iustice of Peace
Mr Christopher Spruce Son to M^{ris} mumble.
M^{r} wild his companion.
M^{r} wellcome brother to M^{ris} mumble.
Strife a lawyer

---

women
M^{ris} mumble a deafe rich widow
Sophia her daughter
m^{ris} wellcome.
Constance Thriftyes daughter.
Iennet Parchm$^{t(}$ wife Thriftyes house keeꝑ.
Cruches wife
Sheepheards
Constable, & officers
Country men & women

Dick Crisp a barber
Spruces man.
Iony wilds man.
Peter Parchm^{t}
Thriftyes Clerk.
Will Catch
Tom Snap
2 theeues
Ned Careles
Iack Killman
Hodge Dingthrift
3 other theeues.
Godfrye.
Cruch an old
country man

Prologue.

Sad stories are the ground work tragedie
Selects to build‸⌜on;⌝; & a well ver'st eye
In works of graue historians onely can
See how the skill of a tragedian
Doth prosecute particulars, how farr
His imitation can be regular
And where it leaues the bookes authority.
So strict a method the solemnity
Of this day doth disclayme, & to be free
From censure takes such spacious liberty
As will not be subordinat to sence
Of any but a [cleare] ⌜strong⌝ intelligence
In wch a modest ingenuity

12 *Thriftyes*] *y* over *e* 20 *build*‸] caret positioned under *d* ⌜*on;*⌝*;*] duplication of punctuation as in MS

Claymes share & fauour, tis humility
To recognize & challenge. Doe but referr
Thingꝭ to their apt relations, challenger
Becomes a vanquisht prisoner, & the man
That was thus humbled, shall triumph againe
Vpon vnable censurers; the fate
Of playes lyes thus, nor is't vnfortunate
To giue some tastꝭ dislike, the publique stage
Is free to all, but ominous p^{r}sage
Rises from iudgem^{t}, wch can onely be
The [clea] cleare discerner of abilitye.

[Fol. 105 p. 1]

1
Enter m^{r} Thrifty, & m^{r} Spruse. **talking togeth^{r}.** 105

Thri: S^{r} I desire yo^{u} to forbeare [to] pressingme further, till I haue
bett^{r} informd my selfe of∧⌜some⌝thingꝭ I am yet vnsatisfied in.
Sp: If by a zealous importunitie
I seeme immodest, tis [the obiectꝭ]∧⌜yor daught^{r}ꝭ⌝worth
That makes me press thus earnestly; & I
Am confident yo^{u} rather [try the heat] ⌜do deferr⌝
yor oft implord assent, to set an edge
[To]∧⌜On⌝appetite w^{ch} [is impossible] **although impossible**
To be made more acute, then cruelly
[subuert me & my fortunes,] [⌜deny my sui⌝]
To deny my suit, & by a sad subu^{r}sion
Ruine me & my fortunes.
Thri. [mast^{r} spruce]
[[I tell yo^{u} againe, we men in authority [⌜comission⌝] do consider much,]]
[[Tis granted by o^{r} com]]
[we haue authority by commission to consider, I to consi=]
[der determine & execute, now the three actions are to]
[be ꝑformd by parties ioyntly [&] ⌜or⌝seuerally, as yor considera=]
[c̃on is to be done by my selfe ꝑ se, or wth my brother *Iusti=*]
[ces cum alijs, the determination, onely by the aduise⌜consent & assent⌝ of]

42 *[clea]*] *a* only partly formed 44 *talking togeth^{r}*] slightly higher placement on line and more sprawling hand suggests late revision; attribution to Hand B not entirely certain 45 *pressingme*] *ing* squeezed in 48 *obiectꝭ]∧*] caret positioned under *ct* 52 *w^{ch}*] perhaps cancelled; penstroke extends under superscript *ch*, but not to *w* 54 *[⌜deny my sui⌝]*] interlined above *subuert me* 58–75 *[[I tell ... plesure]* cancelled with vertical and diagonal hatchings; 58–9 further struck out with horizontal cancellation 61 *execute*] *u* over *t*

[my *Clerk* Peter Parchm^{t} & my selfe, [the execution by]]
[(for yo^{u} know euer a sufficient Clerk lookes [euer] in the]
[statute booke to [know] ⌜see⌝ what his m^{r} may doe, & executi=]
[on by the Constable bedle hang man or‸ ⌜some⌝ such ordinary]
[rascall therefore I say I will consider good m^{r} spruse]
[I will consider.]

[*Sp.* S^{r} do but please to giue me free ꝑmission]
[To lay my seruice at yor daughters feet]
[Till yo^{u} shall think expedient by resolue]
[To answer me or to appoint a day]
[when I may know yor plesure]

Thrif. I say againe
A man in a calling must not neglect his calling,
Let me see. Peter, Peter, [*Ent*]
[Do] *Enter Peter Parchm^{t}*

pulls out his Almanack

Pet. Do's yor worꝑ call.
Thrif. Istnot appointed so!
Pet. How an like yor worꝑ. ***Thrif:* Looke there. Tuesday high wayes**
[*Thrif.* Tue[sday highwayes, Thursday, Alehouses],]
[[*Pet.*] [No sure S^{r} friday Alehouses euer, & though the recogni-]]
***Pet.* no S^{r}. yor booke is false. *Thriftye.* Then prithee mend it.**

[Fol. 105v p. iv]

[sance be forfeit for dressing [meat] ⌜flesh⌝ on a friday, yet]
[it is no matter, the goodwife dos but offend the [king] ⌜law⌝]
[to please the right worꝑfull, but fridaye's the day]
[I [assure yo^{u}] S^{r}.]
⌜So now thus stands the apointm^{t}, munday we meet about ye ou^{r}⌝
Thrif. [Then my booke is false, here mend it, well then]
⌜seers accountƈ, Tuesday sessions,⌝ [⌜munday & we sitt o the⌝]

81 *Istnot*] first *t* squeezed in 83–4 *[Thrif … recogni-]]*] struck out in part and further cancelled with single vertical line 85 *Pet. … it.*] squeezed onto bottom of page 86–9 *sance … S^{r}.*] cancelled with three vertical lines 90–96 *So … alehouses*⌝] original reading: *Then my booke is false, here mend it, well then | thus stands the appointm^{t} wensday Peter thou | knowest is my ⟨ ⟩areing, Tuesday high wayes | Thursday alehouses* [revised to *bridges*], *friday bridges* [revised to *alehouses*]. After this, *wensday Peter thou | knowest is my ⟨ ⟩areing* is cancelled and *munday & we sitt o the subsidye* [revised to *the sessions*] is interlined. In the next stage, *So now thus stands the apointm^{t}, munday we meet about ye ou^{r} | seers accountƈ*, is interlined above cancelled *Then my booke is false, here mend it, well then | thus stands the appointm^{t} munday & we sitt o | the sessions*, *sessions* (94) is interlined above and before *Tuesday*, and *wensday* is interlined before *high wayes* to produce: *So now thus stands the apointm^{t}, munday we meet about ye ou^{r} | seers accountƈ | sessions Tuesday, wensday high wayes*; *sessions Tuesday* then cancelled and *Tuesday sessions,* is interlined above and to the right of *accountƈ*, (perhaps for clarity?). Final reading: *So now thus stands the apointm^{t}, munday we meet about ye ou^{r} | seers accountƈ, Tuesday sessions, wensday high wayes Thursday bridges, friday alehouses.* 92 *[⌜munday … the⌝]*] interlineation begins in MS above *wensday* at 93 as substitution for *wensday … thou*

[thus stands the appointm^{t}] [wensday Peter thou]
[⌜subsidye⌝⌜the sessions⌝][⌜**sessions**⌝]⌜wensday⌝
[knowest is my ⟨ ⟩areing,] [Tuesday]‸ high wayes
Thursday [alehouses] ⌜bridges⌝, friday [bridges] ⌜alehouses⌝, & Saturday bastard
children, S^{r}‸ ⌜all⌝ my time is taken vp, & yo^{u} must wait
my lesure, or let yor suit fall.

[*Sp.* please yo^{u} S^{r} then as I before intreated]
[To giue the tender of my seruice leaue]
[To wait vpon the excellence of her]
[you re blest in being father to.]

[*Thrif:*] [I mu No S^{r}] ***Sp.* Giue me but leaue till you can be at leysure**
To wayt on her you are blest in being fath^{r} too.

Thrif: I must consider of that too, Peter knowes we euer
Take time to consider.

Pe: Euer S^{r} yo^{u} destroy the grauitye of Iustice
els, & make yor authority contemnd.

[*Thrif.* yo^{u} here what [he saith; & he is very well acquain=]]
[[ted wth‸ ⌜the maner of⌝ my ꝓceedingꝭ]]
⌜***Thrif.*Heare you that S^{r}.**⌝

Sp. The two ꝓpitious heralds of success
Hope & Desireous expectation
shall feed my wishes, onely I beseech yo^{u}
[⌜liue still⌝] ⌜**but haue the least [po] roome in yor thoughtꝭ**⌝
Let me [remaine] [recorded in yor memory]
As yo^{u} shall find I merit

⌜***Thrif.*** **m^{r} Spruce you must be satisfyed or authoritye shall silence you.**⌝

[*Pet:*] [S^{r} you're too mild, giue him a check & leaue him.]
⌜**Come letꝭ be gon Pet^{r}.**⌝

[*Thrif*] [m^{r} Spruse I tell yo^{u} yo^{u} must be satisfied or autho=]
[rity [must] ⌜shall⌝ silence yo^{u}, S^{r} I assure yo^{u} aft^{r} the]
[Lords, I am the fift man in comission, & did euer]

94 *[⌜subsidye⌝⌜the sessions⌝]*] two clearly separate interlineations cancelled with single penstroke *[⌜sessions⌝]⌜wensday⌝*] gap between interlineations more pronounced in MS; *sessions* interlined between ⟨ ⟩*areing,* and *Tuesday*; *wensday* interlined with caret between *Tuesday* and *high wayes* 95 ⟨ ⟩*areing*] initial letters obscured by descenders on *sessions* in previous line; perhaps *ordareing*, but not recognized by *OED* 97 *S^{r}*‸] caret positioned under *r* 99–102 *Sp. . . . to.*] cancelled with four diagonal lines through dialogue 103–4 *Sp . . . too*] squeezed into gap created by short cancelled line 107 *Pe:*] *S.* cancelled and *Pe:* over *p.* to alter *Sp.* to *Pe:* 109–10 *[Thrif. . . . ꝓceedingꝭ]]*] struck out in part, and further cancelled with three vertical lines 111 *Thrif.Heare*] speech prefix runs into *H* of *Heare* 122 ⌜*shall*⌝] interlineation not cancelled

[sit next the iudge o the right hand till 2 barronetꝭ]
[of less meanes layd out their mony to make me]
[remoue; there I was wth him Peter. Come.] *Exeunt.*
[*Pet.* [There's a bob for yor [father] [⌜kinred⌝], & so we leaue‸⌜yo^{u}⌝] [yo^{u} in quoꝝ]]
[[Though my m^{r} be not yet I am a Clerk oth' quoꝝ.] *Ex.*]
Sp: O Stupidity in the robes of Iustice, thy Clerks eccho,
& the alewiues patron, the beggers torm^{t} & the iay=
lors freind, the whores ꝑsecutor, yet thyn‸⌜owne⌝ minds
baud, thou seller of Iustice, & buyer of capons wth
the breach of thyne oath & betrayeing of thine own

[FOL. 106 p. 2]

vnderstanding of less extent then thy conscience 2
[now thou hast a daughter I wish thee gelded] 106
How miserably plagud is my deare *Constance* to
haue such a thing to her father as cannot read
english but in his Clerks hand nor euer writ
[⌜once when Parchmt was out oth' way vpon cap paꝑ⌝]
suꝑscription but to the Constable & his deputy
⌜& that vpon cap paꝑ.⌝

Dr S. this speech not so cleare & ꝑspicuous

[*Sp.*] Hath heauen vouchafd to bless the fruitfull earth
wth opulency & denyd man [liberty] **licence**
⌜when his [hungry] ⌜eager⌝ palat⌝
To [crop] [take it] make it vsefull [for his own necessity]
Is [all most] hungerstarud wth the extremitie
Of leane defect. hath plenteous nature
[(For patience will not beare more similes)]
[Hath she I say] ⌜descended to⌝ enlighten[d] mans capacity
wth a peculiar singlenes of obiect
Clearer in essence, & in opposition
Then the app^{r}hensiue sence [it] [wch did p^{r}sume] ⌜to wch it was⌝
[To make it passiue,] [& in that ꝑfanation] [⌜for that offence⌝]

126 *Exeunt.*] *eunt.* over *it* 127 ⌜*yo^{u}*⌝] single penstroke cancelling *There's ... leaue* angles upward to include this interlineation. Order of revisions: *kinred* interlined to replace *father* and *yo^{u}* interlined with caret to replace *yo^{u} in quoꝝ*; two-line speech (127–8) then struck out, and further cancelled with hatchings *[yo^{u} in quoꝝ]*] superscript *u* separately cancelled 128 *oth'*] apostrophe unclear; apostrophe loops away from, rather than towards, *h* 131 *thyn*] *n* squeezed in 138–66 *Dr S. this speech not so cleare & ꝑspicuous*] *Dr S.* written in ink; *this ... ꝑspicuous* written originally in pencil and traced over in ink. Hand uncertain, but black ink resembles that used for late-stage revisions 105r–106v. 139 *Parchmt*] *ar* over *et* 144 ⌜*eager*⌝] positioned above cancelled *hungry* 145 *[for ... necessity]*] cancelling penstroke below passage 152 ⌜*to ... was*⌝] interlined above *w^{ch} ... p^{r}sume* 153 *[⌜for ... offence⌝]*] interlined above *& ... ꝑfanation*

[yeelded & so] Accounted passiue; & yet in strict[nes] ⌜reuenge⌝
of [o^{r}]‸ ⌜my⌝ vnworthy valueing that [prize] [price] **gem**
⌜**mine eyes had glimpse of but their amazd pupills**⌝
[w^{ch} [we] did striue to reuerence yet could not]
⌜**Durst not examine, interposed a cloud**⌝
[serue in ꝑfection, cast a cloud between]
⌜**Between**⌝ [Vs] ⌜me⌝ [&] [o^{r}] [⌜my⌝] ⌜**& my**⌝ blessing. yes [she hath], tis yeelded.
I call the starrs to witnes thingꝭ go wrong
In nature, for the sublim'd eminence
Transcends my knowledge & let me not be punisht
That I [reach at yet not attaine the pitch] ⌜**contend to striue that loftye pitch**⌝
my extended nerues endeauour [yet]‸ [⌜and⌝] ⌜**but power**⌝ come**s**short of
Constance is pure, grant a religious preist
Adores her as a goddess, ⌜&⌝ ꝑformes
The holy rites [zelous] deuotion [calls for] ⌜can inuoke⌝
Tis smoke that rises, & though it be a ꝑfume
Enricht wth prime extractions, yet it is
But vapour or the excrem^{t} of gum̃
Offerd to clearenes, wch will meet as euen
[(But that her] [courteous‸ fauour] [⌜mercye⌝] [takes cõpassion)]
As a clowns morrice at a masque at court
Or cipress apples at a nuptiall feast
And since yo^{u} are so good, shall ⌜therefore⌝ shall I
That think yor praises, farr too low to speake 'hem

[FOL. 106V p. 2V]

Be slighted by yor father who's[is] [so] ⌜to yo^{u}⌝
As mustles are to curious waterd pearles
[⌜vgly themselues yet are in some esteeme⌝]
[W^{ch} shine[s] farr more ꝑspicuously faire]

154 *Accounted*] *A* uncertain; shows exaggerated initial flourish 155 *that*] *at* over *e*, using blacker ink than found elsewhere on page *gem*] probably written by Hand B, but insertion too short for certainty 156 *mine*] *m* over *I*. Probable order of revisions: *we* at 157 cancelled and *I* interlined above using same brown ink; 157 then cancelled and *mine . . . pupills* interlined in darker ink over *I* 160 ⌜*Between*⌝] interlined under *Vs* ⌜*& my*⌝] interlined; probably written by Hand B, but insertion too short for certainty. Probable order of revisions: *Vs* and *o^{r}* cancelled and *me* and *my* interlined above using same brown ink; ampersand presumably cancelled at next stage when *Between* and *& my* introduced by Hand B 163 *my*] over *o^{r}*; superscript *r* scribbled out 165 *[yet]‸*] caret positioned under *et* ⌜*but power*⌝] positioned directly to right of interlined *and* *comesshort*] first *s* squeezed in; distinctive Hand B form 167 *goddess*] *ss* over *s* 173 *courteous‸*] caret positioned under first *u* *[⌜mercye⌝]*] positioned with caret as substitution for cancelled *courteous fauour*; 173 with its interlineation subsequently cancelled 176 ⌜*therefore*⌝] intended placement marked by thin line extending from terminal *e* down between *shall* and *shall* 178 *who's[is]*] *'s* squeezed in

⌜So vgly that they are not worth the touching⌝
[When [in a] o^{r} consideracõn repeates]
⌜much less a carefull eyes inspection⌝ [lustre]
[From whence they came] [Cleare starr thy glorious]‸
⌜But for [thy] their rich childs worth,⌝
[pierces a muddie [⌜cloud⌝] & will appeare]
[At noone in Sun shine] ⌜Appeare thy selfe,⌝
I scorn to make my way by such a ꝑson
[That] ⌜As⌝ will abuse both Emperess & sub^{t}
My thoughtꝭ outrun my hast, [they] ⌜and⌝ both shall‸ [⌜striue⌝] be
[wth a con] Ambitious in contencion, onely to thee.

Enter m^{r} wild

Hitherto corected in this ⟨b⟩ooke from this place in the other.

wild. What to me Kit ha?
Sp. I spoke not to yo^{u}.
wild. To whom then prithee dost thou vse to talk
when nobody is in the roome but thy selfe.
Sp. I vse it not, nor would I take exception
Should yo^{u} desire in a [rese] retired priuacy
To vent those troubleous sighes, whose [hard]‸ ⌜close⌝ retentiõ
would crack a rim of steele.
wild. I thank my starrs S^{r}, Bansted is more
auspicious then so, ⌜two matches &⌝ three forfetures in one
weeke, prety trading, thus yo^{u} see mony
comes in S^{r}, & nothing but want of that can
make me sigh, but no such sighes my little
spruce as to breake ribbs of steele, fy vpon
those sighes Kit fye.
Sp. may they not trouble yo^{u} from my heart I
wish.
wild. Take no care take no care‸ ⌜man⌝ I warrant thee, but
do yo^{u} heare S^{r} though I am an elder brother yet
no Iustice of peace‸ ⌜Ile examine yo^{u} & yo^{u} must⌝ tell me whatꝭ the reason
why yo^{u} made a fantastick eleuation
Of all yor optick nerues, & did contend
[wth earnestnes to make a dilatation] ⌜To manifest by serious protestation⌝

184 *[lustre]*] turned-over line in MS 189 *my*] *w* altered to *m* *such a*] small curl to right of *a* 194 ⟨*b*⟩*ooke*] reading very uncertain. Letter better resembles Hand B's secretary *h* or long *s* rather than rounded italic *b*; *booke* offers best sense in context 200 *[hard]*‸] caret positioned under *r* 203 *three*] *r* over *e*

⌜yor selfe a foole. for [thus]∧∧ ⌜in this tone⌝ [yo^{u} spoke] [& I]⌝∧ ⌜yo^{u} spoke⌝
[Of the eyes pupill, [as] to no other end]∧
[But∧ ⌜t⟨o⟩⌝ shew yor selfe an amorous foole]
[As boyes mak]
And I [did] neuer knew yo^{u} were a randing player

[Fol. 107 p. 3]

107 3.

Till yor own heat of passion did discou^{r}
yor weakenes by the loudnes of yor voice
Dost think it do's become thee & me to talke
Venus orta mari, & so her disposition was &c.
Or to cry the blind [blo] boy has killd a gamster?
Is't possible the singing of *Cupids* arrowes
should be heard at [m^{ris} yardlyes] [an ordnary] ⌜m^{ris} yardlyes⌝
where [euery] ⌜most⌝ men that come[s] haue [had as many] ⌜known the⌝
⌜difference of com̃odities, & [known] ⌜discerne⌝ thingꝭ frõ thingꝭ⌝
[whores as there are chances.] ⌜as playnely as chances⌝
Sp. yo^{u} are absurd
wild. But∧ ⌜yo^{u} think⌝ tis very com̃endable to guarb yor selfe
to a posture as yo^{u} were acting Hamlet, [or]
[think] ⌜& are of opinion⌝ yo^{u} ꝓfane loue to name it except yor
hand keep time o yor brest & [⌜you⌝] not looke down=
ward but of necessity then twist yor band
string or pull yor hat downe, thus, nay mark
me, [or] ⌜and⌝ if yo^{u} will ha yor selfe abusd to the pur=
pose, obserue my prologue & then enter Kit
spruse.
Sp. Thourt tedious in fooling, & it becomes thee
scuruily,
Could I but weigh the noblenes of passion
wth equall counterpoise, or find a parallell

217 ⌜*yor ... spoke*⌝] ⌜*yor ... spoke*⌝ interlined with caret after *end* at 218; *thus* then hatched out and ⌜*in ... tone*⌝ interlined above and slightly to the right of *yo^{u} spoke* with two carets after *thus* to mark placement; *yo^{u} spoke* then cancelled and written in after ⌜*in ... tone*⌝ with another caret to clarify intended position; *& I* then cancelled and repositioned in left margin at 221 *[thus]∧∧*] first caret positioned under *u*, second after *s* 219 ⌜*t⟨o⟩*⌝] perhaps cancelled, but blot obscures second letter and possible cancellation 221 *knew*] *e* over *o* 227 *blo*] small ink mark to right of *o*; presumably the start of the next letter of the incomplete and cancelled word 228 *singing*] ink blot over most of word 229 *[m^{ris} ... yardlyes*⌝] *m^{ris} yardlyes* hatched out, *an ordinary* written on line immediately after then cancelled, *m^{ris} yardlyes* interlined above *an ordinary* 230–2 *where ... chances*⌝] Original reads *where euery man that comes haue had as many | whores as there are chances.*; *man* altered to *men* with *e* over *a*; *as playnely as chances* (232) interlined below *whores ... chances.* 237 *[⌜you⌝]*] lettering smudged and very faint; reading uncertain

To set ag^{t} the dearenes of affection
I am inuolud in.

wild. Then the fruitfull earth
would not be cruell to afford man plenty
And yet deny it; then abounding nature
words
would be as iust as bounteous, (mark yor own)
Not a gem
should be layd out to feed the m^{r}chantꝭ eye
And yet he dye a bankrupt. Now I m out
But tis no matter, this manifestꝭ thy foolery∧⌜sufficiently⌝
Make a behoouefull vse on't & [be wise.] [not]
scratch∧⌜not⌝ thy head as if all thy fortunes lay onely vp=
on the legall inioyeing, of [wom⟨e⟩n] vanity emblemd

[Fol. 107v p. 3v]

in a peculiar of the brittle sex.

Sp. [It]∧⌜A desꝑate malady⌝ seemes an easy cure
⌜the [healthfull]∧⌜[strong big bon'd] sinowye⌝ clown condemns⌝
To men in [health]⌜strength⌝, [to haue a desperate malady]
The courtiers riot, when his want of health
Comes onely by a vigilant attendance
Vpon his prince, sollicitous nightwachingꝭ
Oft [brea] wast the strength of n̄re, when the man
That beares the [inconuenie]⌜[needf] ineuitable⌝ mischeefe is imputed
disorderly deboyst, & do not yo^{u} taxe
me wth [vnworthy]∧⌜effeminate⌝ carriage, because my thoughtꝭ
[Do shew] ꝑforme an homage in their meditation
To a sole peece of vertue in whose wor^{p}
If I [extinguish or] consume∧⌜or do burn out⌝ my selfe
[As s] As incense layd vpon a sacred altar
I shall be blessed in the dedication
Of such a sweet consumption.

252 *words*] turned-over line in MS 260 *[wom⟨e⟩n]* scored out and heavily blotted; *e* may read *a* (*e* perhaps over *a* or *a* over *e*) 262–4 *[It] . . . malady*] original passage elliptically reads *It seemes an easy cure* | *To men in health, to haue a desperate malady*. *It* hatched out and *A desꝑate malady* interlined; *health* cancelled and *strength* interlined; *to . . . malady* cancelled and *the healthfull clown condemns* interlined; *healthful* cancelled and *strong big bon'd sinowye* fitted above with caret; *strong big bon'd* cancelled. Final reading: *A desꝑate malady seemes an easy cure* | *To men in strength, the sinowye clown condemns* Line 263 begins after *y* of *malady* 267 *prince*] inkblot partly obscures *e* 268 *man*] *a* over *e* 271 *[vnworthy]*∧] caret positioned under *th* ⌜*effeminate*⌝] *min* lacks one minim

wild. Stoutly resolud
And wisely worded‸ ⌜I⌝ would I had thy picture,
yo^{u} ha [seene] ⌜heard how⌝ *Narcissus* [picture courting it selfe] ⌜courted his shadow⌝
In the water, & ha‸ ⌜seene a⌝ monkie make loue to a Lady,
[One was made] & what followd, one was made
a flower for his foolery, but the ƀre aduised mon=
ky scratcht the coy deuice by the face, & was
satisfyed, canst not thou doe so?

Sp. Do not ꝓfane those [holy rites I must] [⌜vowd dues I must⌝] ⌜ceremonious dues⌝
my heart hath humbly vowd to ꝓstitute
Before [to] her I [will] adore *Exit.*

wild. Learnedly foold, how ill it becomes a fellow y^{t}
has seene the world to make an ass of himselfe.

Enter Ionye.

Iony. S^{r} the gray neg is sadled, please yor wor^{p} to
go of ayreing tis full time.

wild. Iony I must send thee of a little busines before,
& then twill be time enough.

Iony. Time eneugh S^{r}, ya[^{u}] wad needs ha ya^{r} will & tha
neg's ta law allredy, I ha led on the thick bo=
dy cleth tha he had mere need ha gen wth=
out cle[']s, pre S^{r} ge or le me gang wth him.

[Fol. 108 p. 4]

4

the neg's a flew neg, & had need be atᶜ meet‸⌜againe as soone as may be⌝.

wild. Is fenek ready to? 108

Iony. ya mary is he S^{r}, & the black barbary te, the
gre neg for me, & yo^{u} may rade of ether oth' toth^{r}
but ya may not come oth' gray negs back for ma=
ring his mouth, onles it‸ ⌜be⌝ whan he rakes.

wild. may I not gallop him twelue score or so.

Iony. Ne mary may ye nat till I ha satled his mouth,
sike an ill horseman as ye, may soone spaile a
neg warth mickle mony, come S^{r} will ya gang.

286 *[holy ... dues*⌝] cancelled *vowd ... must* interlined above cancelled *holy rites I must*; *ceremonious dues* interlined below *holy rites I must* 291 *Ionye*] inkblot partly obscures *e* 296 *ya[^{u}]*] *a* probably over *o* 299 *pre*] tiny caret-like mark slightly above and between *r* and *e*. 'Kit Sp⟨ ⟩s' is scribbled below *pre* in very faint pencil on a slight upwards angle; both words are smudged. *gang wth*] small blot followed by horizontal squiggle between *gang* and *wth* 308 *nat*] *a* over *o* 310 *neg*] *e* over *a*

wild. Dost not think Iony the black barbary would be
an incounter for hering.

Iony. Had a little S^{r} you're too swipper, he s bath a win=
ded yan & a men swuft yen, but for Constable
Trap Terwit, Daws [Peggabrig or] Kildeere‸⌜or Peggabrig⌝ at a
single course, aw'syar awne, S^{r}, & Liddell I think ya
wad beet hard Hawden, but war Robin, He's a pla=
gy ape, & at a climm runs windedly, & Hawksworth
oremast^{r}ℓ ye wi speed, yet so I ma rade, Id stren
him sare, tis wary mickle whare to run & whare
to [ca⟨ ⟩k] take a grips‸⌜ats heed⌝, wch the Southern men
[know]‸⌜ken⌝ not; I was brought vp wi Lory Spence, &
he was a men gud keeꝑ, & rad vary weele mary.

wild Then these I may deale wth safely.

Iony ⟨ ⟩ Ist councell ye what te de, send me to make
the match, & le ye down the mony, [&] an I can
get but ⌜halfe⌝ a stene ads a weight, & run at bansted
[Lincoln] or kibblingcotes, Ist de well eneugh wi
Hering, ha's a vary high lewking theife, & tha
ha be winded of a flat, yet he runs best at an
Inwill, & good horsemen think a hill will choke
him, if we can ere lay sides te him, & Ist a war=
rant wth that adds a weight afore I run a mile
Ist [lay sides to him,] be as swuft as he, & if he

[Fol. 108v p. 4v]

be [ether] ⌜euer⌝ masterd wi speed, hes gen, [curbs]
[beat him at Couentry, & he's but a iade for any]
[thing but following hunds]

wild. [mee] Go yo^{u} abroad wth yor horse, & come to me at
the Phenix Tauern, there will be gamsters will
fly at all.

Iony. And I's vp haded ye we's gar hem rue it.

Enter m^{ris} mumble., Spruse, | *Exeunt.*
& Sophia atthe other dore.

314 *Constable*] *C* over *c* 315 *Terwit*] *T* over *t* [*Peggabrig*] *P* over *p* 316 *aw'syar*] *'s* squeezed in (Osborne *s*) 321 *ca*⟨ ⟩*k*] reading uncertain, perhaps *c* 324 *deale*] probably *a* over *e*; reading difficult to make out 325 ⟨ ⟩] smudged passage of approximately four letters; last letter might be *I* 329 *lewking*] *w* oddly formed and may have been adapted from *o* 333 *afore*] *r* over *e* 341 *vp haded*] penultimate *d* blotted, or perhaps written over another letter 343 *atthe*] words run together in MS

Sp. How do yo^{u} forsooth.
mum. Sure tis not so farr ith day.
Sop. my brother ask't yo^{u} how yo^{u} did forsooth.
mum: I wench I, I heare him well, he rises be=
times & thinks tis eight a clock when tis
but breake of day; but let him say what he
will tis not so late
Sp. How do's this moyst weather agree wth yo^{u} for=
sooth?
mum. Did not I say as much, because now I am in
yeares & ly somwhat long a bed thy brother
playes the knaue wth his aged mother, fy
son Christopher, yo^{u} must come to this.
Sp: Truly forsooth I was onely inquisitiue of
yor health, & I hope yo^{u} are not offended
at that.
mum. yo^{u} are not wthout yor scuse dos he say true
Sophia?
Sp. Because I loue yo^{u} do not blame me mother
A necessary curse must fall on him
That doth neglect much more abuse his parentℯ.
Sop: As I am modest forsooth, he did but ask
How the cold aire agreed ⌜wth⌝ you, & why yo^{u} walk
wthout yor sables cloke?
mum. A good yeare on him & my blessing too, giue
me thy hand deare Kit, my want of heareing
makes me mistrust but euery sound y^{t} hũms.
A geldor blowes his horn.

[Fol. 109 p. 5]

109 5

The Sheriffe as he goes to th'assises ist not.
yo^{u} do not heare me? do's nether of yo^{u} heare
me? ⌊*Blowes the horne againe like a gelder.*
Has he two or fowre trumpeters *Sophia*, do
yo^{u} not heare, yo^{u} are more deafe then I.
Sp. We heard before forsooth but were vnwilling
[B] To let yo^{u} know what great mistakes yo^{u} run‸ ⌜intto⌝

358 &] blotted; possibly over blotted *a* 376 *trumpeters*] *ers* over *r* *do*] *o* blotted; perhaps should read *doo*

By yor imꝑfect heareing.
mum. Though my heareing faile, my memory do's
not, I may mistake when yo^{u} speake to me
a word or so, but I remember the sound
of a trumpet, & that noyse wthout is sure the
Sheriffes trumpeters;
Sop. No truly forsooth.
mum. The Kingꝭ trauelling players then are they?
for theres fowre or fiue at least.
Sop. Nether tis a single sow gelder, that blowes
his horn for work.
mum. Out minks let my hand goe‸ ⌜Kit⌝ that I may cud=
gell her wth both hands, will yo^{u} learn to lye
so young?
Sp. As I loue yo^{u} mother yo^{u} mistake, my sister
told yo^{u} true
mum. Then I see I decay, yet I can drink pretyly
well still, & sleepe indifferent & feele rarely
[*She neezeth & breakes wind*
Both. Bless yo^{u} mother.
mum. Breakeing wind eases an old woman extremly
But as I told yo^{u}, I can drink & sleep well &
feele very well still, & a good feeling is that w^{ch}
deafe blind & lame must trust to, & may liue well
if they want not that.
Sp. I am glad to see yo^{u} so well disposed forsooth.
mum. yes the more is my harm it has more fayld
me of late, since the last trayneing I ha
been much deafer, & yet I neuer go wthout
black wooll.

[FOL. 109V p. 5V]

Sp. yo^{u} right yor selfe, & [do] ⌜take⌝ compassion[ate] ⌜of⌝
yor freinds & children by makeing vse of meanes
To p^{r}serue yor selfe.
mum. yo^{u} say true Kester, Sack is exceeding good too
Especially for those that are troubled as I am
for my greefe comes of a cold cause, & any

384 *that*] *at* over *e*   409 *black*] *b* over letter that is perhaps *c*

warm thing nourishes.
Sop: Shall I make ye a caudle forsooth?
mum. yes good wench I heard y^{t} very well.
And p^{r}pare my cullis & my hartƈ horn gelly
ag^{t} my vsuall howres; & let Bridget my chamber=
maid warm my mase ale & bring it i the∧⌜siluer tankard [of a]⌝ [quart]
[pot]∧⌜that holds a quart⌝, I think now I ha fasted so long I can ouer=
come such a small quantity tis a speciall good
thing for the wind [especially]∧⌜if a body can take⌝ great draughtƈ. *Ex Sophia.*
Sp. Now will I try if she can heare me.
mum. Take me by th'arme kit, though [me thinks] my
heareing be rather better then worse wth walking
yet me thinks my head is som what dizzy.
Sp. Want of vse mother yo^{u} can not mend in all
places at once, I am glad yor heareing mends.
mum. yes I can heare words indifferent well, but
these loud noyses confound me, as yo^{u} saw yor
selfe.
Sp. yo^{u} will not rest forsooth.
mum. O no Kit I loue to talk & will willingly heare
thee if my imp̱fection do not make thee ouer=
strayne thy voice, wth continuance, I loue long tales
dearely, & will be more attentiue, that thy troble
may be the less.
Sp: Poet I was neuer, & a confusd historian
I hate, but if youl heare a modern accident
Such as my memory hath bene bold to store vp
I will wthout forestalling it wth censure
playnely deliuer each occurrence to yo^{u}
True iestƈ in my opinion are the best
Though they be bitter, & serious relations
Loose more then halfe their worth if verity
Be not the midwife to the reporters words.

420 *Bridget*] B over *b* 421–2 *i the ... quart*⌝] original passage reads *i the quart* | *pot*; interlined *siluer tankard of a* positioned with caret before cancelled *quart*; *of a* subsequently cancelled; *that holds a quart* interlined above *pot* with caret positioned under *t* of *pot* 422 *think*] *i* over another letter, probably *a* 425 *try*] *r* over *y* 427 *be*] over *is*

6.

mum. I loue to heare a tale, a part whereof 110
I know to be or not to be my selfe.
Sp. when yo^{u} haue heard the fable I am confident
you'l cry tis so, & so, & morallize
As well as those that were the p^{r}sent witnesses
mum. It may be so begin good Kit begin.
Sp. As the earth hath variety of obiectꝭ
So men of various dispositions
Looke wth dislike or approbation on them,
Some affect sportꝭ, some seriousnes, some like
The warrs, some peacefull carriages, some loue
The pleaseing of [hi] their sight, ⌜&⌝ others satisfy
The more ignoble sences, & all end
In sad repentance, & but that tediousnes
Would seeme to haue the mastry, nay ꝑhaps
Get it ag^{t} o^{r} will, [it is] ⌜twould be⌝ concluded
By the best vnderstandings [onely to thinke] ⌜twere the way⌝
⌜Beyond compare, nay ye prime vndertakeing⌝
Immediatly [on immortalitie],
[If it were not deemd most impossible] ⌜to catch at immortality⌝
Wthout respectiue helps or those conducem^{t}ꝭ
That [helps]∧ ⌜ease⌝ vs in the way, & nere attend
The tedious hand of death, w^{ch}∧ [⌜euer⌝] comes too slowly
To men p^{r}pared. But since mortalitie
Is iudgd & sentencd to a casuall fayling
Nay certaine interruption, & deniall
Of long continuance [to a] in the very word
That signifies [it selfe.] ⌜mortalitye⌝, As a man not denyed
The priuiledges others doe possess
One in a neare degree of consanguinity
To yo^{u} deare mother, valueing chastity
Before impure miscalld delightꝭ, not reall
To those y^{t} vse 'hem, but [onely beneficiall] ⌜exemplary & vsefull⌝
To them that [wth a hate] hate those beastly practises

450 *loue*] penstroke through *o*; probably a slip of the pen 467 *Beyond ... vndertakeing*] full line interlined 471 *[helps]*∧] caret positioned under *ps* 472 *w^{ch}*∧] caret positioned under *h* 473 *To*] *T* over *t* (original *t* also blotted)

Hath not wth ouerualueing selfe loue
Huggd but imployed in a manly way
Affection not lustfull appetite.,
The day was geniall when his first designe
Tooke life, iudiciall Astrologie
Approued‸⌜the season,⌝, the ꝓpitious signe
Stood where he would haue wisht, & eu^{r}y circũ=
(stance

[FOL. 110V p. 6v]

mou'd wth so [great]‸⌜faire⌝ a ꝓbabilitye
Success was yeelding. But then happines
Had come too soone, ꝑfect felicitie
Hath not so quick a generation
Because itꝭ setled ꝑpetuitie
Is of a longer residence. But then
His grasping thoughtꝭ extended soft imbraces
And catchd the interposed rubb wch stayd
Him from a sweet fruition.
Mum. I bless my hearing
And haue not a [great] ⌜long⌝ time heard so ꝑfectly
But yet I vnderstand yo^{u} not
Sp. Then mother
Receaue wth patience, & repay wth opulency
That wch yor child shall tell yo^{u}, since it is
Onely to make his fortunes & yor comfort.
mum. Now I begin to be more deafe againe.
Sp. If I be troublesome I will cease.
mum. No Kit.
Sp. But I shall rayse my voice & speake distinctly
[mum.] yor faire ꝑmission gaue me leaue to make
mine own free choice, I in despite of censure
Setled my mind, the miserable carle
And father to the admirable virgin

484 *ouerualueing*] *ual* over *lau* 488 *life*] *f* over *k* 489 ⌜*the season,*⌝,] duplication of punctuation as in MS 491 *(stance*] positioned as in MS 492 *[great]* ‸] caret positioned under *e* 496 *Because*] *c* over *s* or *f*; descender of original letter largely scraped away 499 *catchd*] *tc* over *ct* 512–23 *[mum.]* ... *mum*] secretary lines facing out and running vertically between speech prefixes reads: [*because ye land*] | *because the land is yo^{r}ꝭ* | [*came all by yo^{u}*] | *for life*. A dagger-like bar with three crossbars runs down from interlined ampersand between *me,* and *I* (517); bar probably positions *& my disability* in place of caret, but possibly might mark placement of marginalia. Sense of passage easier to grasp if one infers full-stop after *disability*.

mainly excepted, at the p^{r}sent maintenance
yo^{u} yearely, giue me, ⌜& my disability⌝ I durst not p^{r}sume
⌜To make my wife a ioynture⌝
To ascertaine him of more, till yor full hand
Should giue me cause, & yor concession
Giue me direction to inform him [so] yo^{u}
Would please to be more liberall.
mum. O Kit now
S I am deafer then at first
Sp. Then Ile speake louder.
mum No as thou louest me, for so I may ꝑhaps
Greeueing my troubled ⌜sence⌝ be made vncapbible
Of euer heareing more
Sp: If I ꝑplexe yo^{u}
Think yo^{u} were yong yor selfe, think yo^{u} were once
As I am now onely the sex excepted,

[FOL. 111 p. 7]

And when I haue wth miserable extasie 111 7
Opend my heart in serious expression,
Ether releeue or ruine me, tis yo^{u}
I liue to serue, & yo^{u} must suffer if
I do miscarry. Do but heare me out
And I shall liue or dy at yor dispose.
mum. I cannot heare, I haue heard while I can,
& a body can do no more then they can, I
was thick of heareing but now Im deafe
deafe as an Adder I & yo^{u} haue made me so
Sp. Ile take the boldnes to express my mind
In writing if my words be so offensiue.
mum. I heare yo^{u} not I tell yo^{u} once againe.
Sp. Be not so wedded to yor own conceipt
As [make] ⌜see⌝ me suffer, when a small ꝓportion
⌜Of what yo^{u} haue⌝ Would make me swell wth plenty
And thank my starrs & yo^{u}, if yo^{u} desire
To haue the Lady nam'd for whose indearem^{t}
I do thus humbly craue yor charity
Tis the desert of *Constance* makes me press y^{u}o

551 *y^{u}o*] *u* pushed back due to space constraints

Whom exception cannot touch.
mum. Kit spruse I tell thee, if I giue thee now w^{t}
wilt thou haue when I die; the wench is a
good crout, I fault her not but if I giue
thee now what wilt thou haue when I die.
Sp. I am glad yor heareing is recou^{r}ed
I will but [vse] ⌜vse⌝ one oth^{r} argum^{t}. —
mum. No o thy mothers word I am deafe still
Very deafe, exceeding deafe passing deafe
extraordinary deafe, deafe deafe deafe.
Sp. Then let me haue yor licence to renounce
my natiue soyle, [s⟨ ⟩] & leaue the place yo^{u} gaue
me my first being in, if such hard heartednes
Liue in a mother, to inforce me to
So violent a course.
mum. I loue thee kit
O do not so my boy
Sp: Why now yo^{u} heare againe
mum. Very little

[Fol. 111v p. 7v]

Sp. Nay then haue at you; what if I in a rage [I]
Should goe [&] hang my selfe, & leaue a paꝑ in
my pocket, or in my hatband wch should express
Christopher Spruse hang'd himselfe because his
moth^{r} would not make his wife a iointure,
were not m^{ris} mumble guilty think [yee] yo^{u}?
mum. Ill words in a boyes mouth, ill words in a boyes
mouth, here take all my keies, but meddle not
wth the box othe right hand in my cabinet for
there lies mercury, when I was yong I vsd
it to make me looke cleare.
Sp. I warrant yo^{u} mother.
mum. But least thou shouldst mistake Ile go along,
an the boy should pawn my diamonds‸ ⌜now⌝, yet let
hem goe, to saue a man & to make a man is
more then euery old woman can doe, take all

563 *[s⟨ ⟩]* reading uncertain; looks like *smi*, but as none of the minims are dotted it might be *sim*

Kit but hang not thy selfe, no more of those
words my boy.

Sp. youl take away the cause, & then th effect
Cannot [Cannot]^ [⌜Will not⌝]succeed. [Children cannot liue] ⌜Liberall & kind⌝
[If their hard parentℯ do refuse to giue]
[⌜Are needfull adiunctℯ to a parentℯ mind⌝]
[Them competencie ⌜&⌝ tis a less offence]
⌜Should [be] ⌜liue⌝ ioynt tenantℯ in a parentℯ mind⌝
[To cloye wth store, then starue wth indigence]

Fin: Act.1. *Exeunt*

Enter Thrifty, m^{ris} Constance, Peter Parchm^{t}
& m^{ris} Iennet.

Thrif: And as I told yo^{u} girle giue no answer of yor own
but if I be out of the way call *Iennet* to coun=
cell & so ꝓceed.

Con. S^{r} I shall in obedience to yo^{u}
Obserue yor strict [iniunctions] ⌜co͂mands⌝, duty binds
And I shall yeeld, my care shall manifest
my duty, & if both can inable me
[To serue yo^{u} as yor] [wish, & my desire[s]] [⌜own directions⌝] [⌜plesure shall⌝]
[Appoint]
To execute yor plesure, no iniunction
That comes from yo^{u} shall [seeme a burden to me] ⌜relish of dislike⌝
Though it seeme harsh to oth^{r} app^{r}hensions.

Thrif. My good girle still, & as I told yo^{u} *Iennet*

[Fol. 112 p. 8]

112 8.

when yor husband & I are abroad about the
co͂mon wealth affaires, let *Constance* sit at
the tables end, but yo^{u} keep the key of the
[wine]^ ⌜sack⌝, for wine is ill for girles, it breeds heat

590 *Cannot ... succeed*] *Will not* interlined above cancelled *Cannot* with caret positioned under *ot*; *Will not* then cancelled, and *Cannot* written in margin 590–5 *Children ... indigence*] original reading: *Children cannot liue* | *If their hard parentℯ do refuse to giue* | *Them competencie tis a less offence* | *To cloye wth store, then starue wth indigence*; *&* interlined after *competencie*. In next stage, *Liberall & kind* interlined above cancelled *Children ... liue*; *Are ... mind* (592) interlined above cancelled *Them ... offence* (*u* of *adiunctℯ* over interlined *&*), then cancelled; *Should be ioynt tenantℯ in a parentℯ mind* interlined above cancelled *To ... indigence*; *be* cancelled and *live* positioned above. Finally revised passage reads, *Liberall & kind* | *Should liue ioynt tenantℯ in a parentℯ mind.* 606–7 *[To ... Appoint]*] original reading: *To serue yo^{u} as yo^{u} wish, & my desires* | *Appoint*; second *yo^{u}* adjusted to *yor* (*r* over *u*), terminal *s* on *desires* cancelled. In next stage, *wish ... desire* cancelled and *own directions* interlined above, then cancelled; *plesure shall* interlined below *wish* and cancelled; finally, *To ... yor* and *Appoint* cancelled
616 *[wine]^*] caret positioned under *n*

i their faces, & then they must lay on black paches
wch they say is all the fashion, but as I told yo^{u}
me thinks tis very scuruy.

Ien. For that forsooth let yor worp^{s} care be at rest
& yor mind at quiet, clarifyed whey is excel=
lent all this time oth' yeare, & though I say
it before her face my yong m^{ris} is very ty=
dy, & passing tractable, [for]

Thrif. The better girle I assure thee

Ien. yes I le ensure yor worp̃, for when her musique
m^{r} was teaching her o the lute she [askt my opi=] ⌜would needs⌝
[nion]‸ ⌜know⌝ wheth^{r} [I thought] ⌜she sate⌝ streight or no, & would
not suffer him to turn ⌜vp⌝ her minikin till she
askt my opinion whether I thought it would
abide streching or no. ,

Thrif: Good agen, good agen, wonderfull good, vpon
my [word &] wor^{p}⌜full word⌝ wonderfull good.

Ien. No indeed forsooth she will not willingly haue
a pin pind about her but I must be at the,
thrusting of it in, nor a knot tyed but I
must spend my censure wheth^{r} it ioyne close
or lye of a lumpe, & so [is]‸ ⌜be⌝ like to offend in the
weareing.

Pet. See, see, how say.

Ien. yes of a certaine

Thrif: yet notwthstanding as I told yo^{u}‸ ⌜*Iennet*⌝, if *Kit spruse*
or any other [the] picture[s] of gallantry chance
to come, & ꝓtest like a gentleman, respect him
worpfully, for I find by my selfe tis not euery
mans case to do gentleman like, & though I
bought my armes of the herald & haue payd
for 'hem too, obserue yo^{u}, that, yet sometimes I dis=

[FOL. 112v p. 8v]

couer my selfe to be a very clowne, & would loose
any thing but my place ith' com̃ission to be as well
fashiond as Kit Spruse, therefore if he come & ꝓtest

624 *[for]*] *f* hatched out; *or* smudged 628 *[nion]*‸] caret positioned under terminal *n* 631 *no.*] hooked shape to right of *no.* (above *d* of *good* at 632) 638 *[is]*‸] caret positioned under *i* 642 yo^{u}‸] caret positioned under *u*

as a gentleman, vse him as a gentleman, thou *Ienet*
in authority.

Pet. S^{r} as yor worp makes bold wth me ⌜in things yo^{u} vnderstand not⌝, [so yo] so I pray
giue me leaue to ask yo^{u} a question. what is it to
ꝓtest like a gentleman.

Thrif. O thou illiterd excrem^{t} of authority, not know y^{t} tis
as essentiall to a gallant to ꝓtest as for thy m^{r} to
call a Constable *Sirrah*, attend & Ile instruct thee.
To ꝓtest like a gentleman is to forsweare a mans
selfe, but that can onely be tried by [the sequell]‸⌜examinatiõ of y^{e} thing⌝, &
so not [so] ꝓ ꝑ for thy p^{r}sent instruction, but to ꝓtest
like a gentleman in breefe is to ꝓtest in short
to ꝓtest at length is to be done in more words
& to ꝓtest like a gentleman is to ꝓtest like a gentle=
man, dost not vnderstand man?

Pet. But how S^{r} I beseech yo^{u} explaine yo^{r}selfe?

Thrif. O how patient is Iustice, & how we men in
office are faine to beare wth the vulgar,.

Pet. Truly S^{r} I vnderstand yo^{u} not.

Thrif: Then answer me a question, what fault is the
ꝓuoker instigator or ꝓcurer in.

Pet. Of what S^{r}

Thrif. Of any thing S^{r}

Pet. As the fault deserues S^{r}.

Thrif: As the fault deserues S^{r}, then *Peter parchm^{t}*
is indebted &c 1^{s} for vrging his m^{r} Iustice
Thrifty to make a gentleman like ꝓtestation
wch is not to be done wthout sweareing fy knaue
indeauour to make thy m^{r} guilty contrary to y^{e} statute
⌜in y^{t} case made & ꝓuided [*Anno:* I ha forgot.]⌝

Pet. wth yor patience S^{r} the ꝓtestation is yet vndefin'd.

Thrif: To fooles it is S^{r}, & for ought I know yo^{u} may be
among them & rightfully the first man in Com̃is=
sion, but I will descend once more to lighten thy
vnderstanding, & therfore a gentleman ⌜like⌝ ꝓtestation

652 *him as*] *s* over *t* 661 *sequell]* ‸] caret positioned under *ll* 668 *patient*] terminal *t* over *ce* 680–1 *contrary . . . forgot.*] late revision to speech; *contrary . . . statute* squeezed onto 680, *in . . . forgot*. interlined below

113

is when a ꝓtestation is made by a gentleman of a 9
good house, els y^{e} gentilitie is illegall & vsurpt, yet
the ꝓtestation may be good enough though the gen=
tility be voyd, [is I say] & I say still such a ꝓtestation
Pet. I an like yor wor^{p}.
Thrif: Such a ꝓtestation being made *forma* & [*materia* sig=] ⌜*modo* good words⌝
[nificant words at Oxford though here not vnderstood] ⌜if vnderstood⌝
I say as I told yo^{u} a gentleman like ꝓtestation is a
gentleman like ꝓtestation, & there's enough.
Ien. Enough of conscience husband.
Thrif. O *Iennet* how do's thy capacity exceed thy husbands
in altitude & ꝓfunditie, in depth & compass iust as
my dagger dos thy penknife^⌜*Peter*⌝, | *One knocks.*
Strangers strangers, yo^{u} three tender yor feallty, y^{t}
who beholds here the gou^{r}m^{t} of a republique, may
[not go]^⌜if he⌝ obserue [here, &] not go away vninstructed.

Enter. Spruse, & Crisp his barber.

Sp. No attendance at the gate of Iustice
Then may I enter & giue no offence.

They 3. all this while cursy to Thrifty.

And, dick Crisp do's the powder come neare the
colour of my haire.
Cris. yes S^{r}; tis a ꝑfect ciuet powder 3^{t} an ounce.
Sp. Do the curles of my periwig turn gracefully?
Cris. As the Lords yo^{u} desired to imitate S^{r}, & me
thinks yor colour is farr more complet
Sp. So I come not short, it is no matter, [how farr] ⌜the further⌝ I
exceed [the more] the better.
Cris. Yo^{r} locks of an equall length too, yet me thinks
a careles [weareing]^⌜cast⌝ of yor haire were better, [&^ they] ⌜for those⌝
y^{t} [were]^⌜weare⌝ theire hayre so set & constraynd the witt*e*
censure [as effeminate.] for effeminacie.
Sp. Name me a statesman that is otherwise | *Crisp pawsed*
Cris. I cannot o the sodayne S^{r}.

693 ⌜*modo* ... *words*⌝] positioned above cancelled *materia sig=* 694 ⌜*if vnderstood*⌝] positioned above *nificant words at* 710 *S^{r};*] semi-colon may be a full-stop imperfectly revised to a comma *ciuet*] *c* over *i* 717 *[weareing]^*] caret positioned under *re* 718 *[were]^*] caret positioned under *re*

Sp. And I cannot admit yo^{u} time to study, therefore conuinc't as thou art attend at the dore & Ile discouer my selfe.

[FOL. 113v p. 9v]

Cris. Wth yor [wo] good leaue S^{r}, I take the boldnes to let yo^{u} know S^{r}, the other parties haire appeares about yor [harme]‸⌜arme⌝, wch in my foolish opinion ought to be conceald.

Sp. True [did] Dick; but now tis hidden; take my cloke Dick tis the last fashion to haue the man carry ye m^{rs} cloke, but go no further then my call may reach yo^{u}. | *Cris. stands of a little* with yor good fauour S^{r}.

Thrif. Mr Spruce, good m^{r} Spruse you'r well amet S^{r} you're well amet.

Sp. I take the liberty S^{r}, & I hope wthout offence to salute yor [daug] daughter;

Thrif: Courtesie will not deny y^{t} to a stranger good Mr Spruse, much less to yo^{u} S^{r}. Mr Spruse I was a little busy in giueing rudim^{t} to my family.

Sp: Please you [not to take it ill] ⌜to haue it so⌝ S^{r}, I shall [wil=] [lingly] wthdraw.

Thrif. Good m^{r} Spruse, the [exam] ⌜words⌝ of old men may do yo^{u} good by way of p^{r}cept, & their carriage as I told yo^{u} may instruct yo^{u} by example as I told yo^{u}‸⌜before⌝, therefore attend & be edifyed wth all my hart good m^{r} Spruse.

Sp. I shall S^{r}. | *This while Sp. drawes neare to Constance & talks wth her.*

Thrif. And as I told you Peter, write yor examina= cõns in a full hand.

Pet. yes ant please yo^{u} S^{r}.

Thrif. That as I told yo^{u} the Clerk of th' sises assistãt may not curse yo^{u} for scribling.

Pet. yes S^{r}.

Thrif. But as I told yo^{u} may plainly read the name of the examinate.

727 *[harme]*‸] caret positioned under *me* 737 *[daug]*] *g* only partly formed 746 *marginal mark*] caret in left margin, angled towards the dialogue, is smudged and very faint *yo^{u}*‸] caret positioned under *u*

Pet. I dare warrant yor wor^{p} Ile write the cheife
words, as taken before yor wor^{p} &c' in text
ꝉres.

Thrif. Oh absurd as I told yo^{u}‸ ⌜before⌝ very absurd, hast thou
not my old Clerk Take alls p^{r}sident?

[Fol. 114 p. 10]

10

Pet. yes S^{r}, & his buckrom bag, wch a gentleman studyed in
⌜heraldry councelld me to weare as a pristine relque of an=⌝
⌜tiquity because of the holes⌝

Thrif: [Prosecute that knaue as I told yo^{u} ꝑsecute]
⌜prosecute those p^{r}sidentꝭ as I told ⌜you⌝ & follow the aduise⌝
[that] of y^{t} buckrom bag.
114

Sp. Lady dos yor father affect these number of
as I told ye's, for grace or fantasticknes?

Con. I shall at another time giue yo^{u} [best] ⌜better⌝ satisfaction.

[*Sp.*] *Thri.* And yo^{u} *Iennet* euer before meales as I told
yo^{u} bring me a cup of sack & a tost.

Ien. I forsooth.

Thrif. That as I told yo^{u}‸ ⌜before.⌝ by ye expulsion of the wind
I may make roome for my meat, That as I
told yo^{u} my stomack being of small capacity
may receiue nutrim^{t} wthout disturbance.

Ien. I haue forsooth moreouer made yo^{u} a diet ale
that will giue yo^{u} ease in all companies, & yor
worp^{s} box is neuer [empty], wthout [*manus*] lo=
singes of mine own makeing, I think yor wo^{p}r
has it now about yo^{u}.

Thrif. Admirable good my *Iennet I* ꝑtest, [if thou beest]
[a whore] thou art [a] vsefull [one] as I am a man
in authority [as I told yo^{u}.] but no more of y^{t}
⌜now.⌝

758 *Pet.*] *Thri* smudged out and *Pet.* over 761 *yo^{u}*‸] caret positioned under *u* 764–6 *, & his … holes*⌝] late revision in slightly darker ink fitted into space provided by Peter's original part-line (*yes S^{r}*); *, & his … studyed in* squeezed onto line, *heraldry … holes* interlined below on two separate lines 767–9 *[Prosecute … bag.]* original reading: *Prosecute that knaue as I told yo^{u} ꝑsecute | that*; revised reading: *prosecute those p^{r}sidentꝭ as I told you* [*you* interlined] *& follow the aduise | of y^{t} buckrom bag* (*prosecute … aduise* interlined and *of … bag* fitted onto line after cancelled *that*) 771 *fantasticknes*] *st* over *n*; smudge directly under *ant* 776 *yo^{u}*‸] caret positioned under *u* 779 *disturbance*] small blot positioned high and to the right of this word 783 *wo^{p}r*] *p* pushed back due to lack of space 787–8 *but … now*⌝] late revision; *but … y^{t}* fitted on line, *now* squeezed in below *in authority*

Ien. O good S^{r}.
[*Thrif.*] [Peter as I told yo^{u}.] [⌜Onely to me wench [as] onely to me wench as I⌝]
⌜told yo^{u} Peter, *Pet:* [if yo^{u} had told me S^{r} it]⌝
[⌜would haue made me haue rubbd but these are⌝]
[*Pet.*] [O S^{r}] [⌜onely iesting words among freinds.⌝]
[⌜iesting words among freinds Peter⌝]
Thrif: [Onely to me *Iennet* onely to me as I told]
[you *Iennet*,] ⌜Come come⌝ obserue yor charge & [ꝓsecute] ⌜follow⌝ yor
instructions; & good m^{r} Spruse as I told
yo^{u}, yo^{u} obserue not the lecture I [gaue] ⌜giue⌝ to
my seruantꝭ but as I told yo^{u} yo^{u} are som=
⌜yo^{u} truss y^{e} quarry before yo^{u} haue⌝
what [busy] ⌜nimble⌝, S^{r}, [yo^{u} are yong, & so was I, & the]
⌜made a faire stooping, & I assure yo^{u} S^{r} I am the⌝
[practick gone I now content my selfe wth]
⌜only man that must cry whoo whoop [S^{r}]⌝
[repetition of the theorick, I assure yo^{u} S^{r} it]
[is I must make or marr yor marketꝭ, & though]
[I can tell in what place] & if yo^{u} neglect me
S^{r} as I told yo^{u} authority will think it fitt in
discretion to [punisth] punish yo^{u} ꝓ *comtemptu*.

[FOL. 114V p. 10V]

Sp. If [for]^ [⌜in⌝] ⌜for⌝ a silent admiration
Of yor words serious grauitie, I seeme
worthy of censure, rep^{r}hend yo^{r}selfe
That so mistake a contemplation
Setled in seruing yo^{u}. or if yo^{u} think
my obseruation was not so attentiue
As yor discourse expected, pardon me
Here stands ⟨ ⟩ [a power that] ⌜a ⟨ ⟩ beauty⌝ tyed me to obseruance
In satisfaction of whose least comãnd

790–6 *Thrif. . . . Iennet,*] dialogue originally reads: *Thrif. Peter as I told yo^{u}.* | *Pet. O S^{r}.* | *Thrif: Onely to me Iennet onely to me as I told* | *you Iennet,*. These four lines are cancelled, and five new lines (790–4) are closely interlined above and below, and cancelled in turn: *Thrif. Onely to me wench [as] onely to me wench as I* | *told yo^{u} Peter, Pet: if yo^{u} had told me S^{r} it* | *would haue made me haue rubbd but these are* | *onely iesting words among freinds.* | *Thrif: iesting words among freinds Peter.* The words *told yo^{u} Peter, Pet:* (791), tightly cramped below the already cancelled *Peter as I told yo^{u}* (790), were almost certainly overlooked for cancellation; *onely* of *onely iesting words among freinds* (793) is interlined under cancelled *O S^{r}*, with rest of line positioned to right of *O S^{r}* 809 *comtemptu*] vertical stroke of first *t* extends down as though to form descender 810 *[for] . . . ⌜for⌝] for* positioned above cancelled *in* which is positioned with caret above cancelled *for* *[for]* ^] caret positioned under *o* 817 *stands* ⟨ ⟩] letter blotted and illegible *a* ⟨ ⟩] letter blotted and illegible

my [wis] life [would] ⌜shall⌝ be [spent as] ⌜powrd out⌝ a sacrifice
[powrd on a holy Altar] ⌜Before her [an] shrine⌝; & the expiring sufferer
merit by dying, [whose] ⌜which⌝ sad solemnitie
will honour her, [& giue] [⌜vouchafe⌝] [him]^ ⌜create him⌝ happines
And add to both,;
Thrif: Hy da yo^{u} studied this S^{r}, did yo^{u} not?
Sp. I could not speake till this S^{t} gaue me vtterance
But now I can declame eternally
So I may haue the libertie to speake
Vpon so braue a theme.
Thrif: Againe? satisfy an old man wthout shewing
the extremitie of power in examination, did
yo^{u} not study that speech:
Sp: I tell yo^{u} S^{r} my tong hath not [*potentia*] ⌜a capacitye⌝
T'express my meaning wth so quick deliu^{r}y
As I conceiue her praises.
Thrif: Nor did yo^{u} not pen it, & then con it ouer & so
as we say & as I told yo^{u} deliu^{r} it.
Sp. No by my seruice wch I dedicate
To yor admired daughter.
Thrif: Then Peter as I told yo^{u}^ ⌜before⌝ Iustice is an Ass &
authority a dull [G⟨ ⟩] fellow, Peter as I told
thee thou knowest, I euer write my charges
learn hem [wthout booke] ⌜by hart⌝, cry *sic Bodinus de Rep*:
am admired by the grand iury, carry away the
credit of the bench, & yet sweat for't afore at
least a month, & take more paines to get it wth
out booke then the poore sheepstealers ⌜doe to haue⌝ *misere=*
re,, ⌜*ad vnguem*,⌝ & now m^{r} *Spruse* put*ẽ* me down ex tempore,
I can assure yo^{u} m^{r} *Spruse* yo^{u} are [as] [little]^ ⌜no more⌝ to be in=

[Fol. 115 p. 11]

115 11

durd then an vnderstanding Iustice amongst
a company of weake fellowes, & so I leaue

819–20 *life ... shrine*] original reading: *life would be spent as a sacrifice* | *powrd on a holy Altar*; revised to read *life shall be powrd out a sacrifice* | *Before her [an] shrine* 825 *till*] *i* over *l* 839 *yo^{u}*^] caret positioned under *u* 840 *[G⟨ ⟩]* approximately two letters smudged out and illegible 845 *paines*] some kind of adjustment at *in* has been made, but revision unclear; *panes* perhaps revised to read *paines* 848 *[little]*^] caret positioned under *tt*

yo^{u} but *Iennet* a care of my girle good *Ien=*
net. [on thy trust] [is my] [I‸ onely rely.] ⌜a care of my girle.⌝ [Come]
[Peter – Good]

Sp. Pray S^{r} abide me but one word before
yo^{u} goe, my suit hath tediously attended
Vpon yor plesure, do not remaine inexorable
But now at last giue me a word of comfort

Thrif: S^{r} as I told you before, as I commit all
matters of Iustice to my clerk, so I do the
affaires of my estate & maching my daughter
to his wife, that whollsome dry nurse m^{ris}
Ienet, that [tolerable] *remediũ* that stands by
yo^{u}, tis true I assure yo^{u}, as I told yo^{u} before
good m^{r} Spruse.

Sp. S^{r} if my short liud memory deceiue me not
yo^{u} neuer told me so before, [thou]‸ ⌜though⌝ yo^{u}
Be pleasd to say yo^{u} did

Thrif: As I told yo^{u} before S^{r} is my word, I am affec=
ted to the phrase S^{r}, & fault me not [thoug] ⌜if⌝ I
lace my discourse wth as I told yo^{u} or as I told
you before, for men in my place euer haue their
words by themselues, & when I was put in com=
mission I made choice of as‸ ⌜I⌝ told yo^{u} S^{r}, there=
fore vnderstand as I told yo^{u} & be satisfyed as
I told yo^{u} before *Exit Thrifty.*

Pet. I beseech yo^{u} S^{r} vse my wife & my yong m^{ris}
well while my m^{r} sleeps I must dispach some
country business. *Exit Peter*

Sp. I rather must desire that courtesy
At both their hands my selfe.

Con. A fathers charge
Limit(my will, [I] ⌜nor⌝ am‸ ⌜I⌝ [not] licencd
Texpress my selfe, yet wth a [hopefull wish] ⌜longing hope⌝
[That] ⌜my⌝ patience may procure me libertye
Ile please my selfe wth thinking what an action
must not giue life to yet.

853 ⌜*a* . . . *girle.*⌝] positioned over *thy* . . . *onely* 870 *[thoug]*] *g* only partly formed

Sp. I had not relisht ioy so sensibly
If opposition had not made it pleaseing.
To want a meale or two instructꝭ a man
How to set value [of]‸⌜on⌝ a liberall feast.
I feard & hop'd, I did assure my selfe
Then sad despaire came sodainly & washt
That faire side of wch made a sweet apparance.
But now the sun begins to be a victor
Faire weather comes wthout the plowmans prayers
Yet he's sole debter whom the benefit
Obligeth to be gratefull. I learn to make
An application, had yo^{u} but smild before
my inward feare had blusht this second ꝑt
Had not bene reall; but the first born fruit
Is euer ꝑfect, & the Stork that giues
His voluntary [bird] ⌜yong⌝ is farr more noble
Then to demand that [bird] ⌜gift⌝ bird back againe.
pardon dread princes of my cogitations
I doe compare in broken sentences
Yo^{u} & these [farr] ⌜much⌝ inferiours, yor smile
Gaue me a courag'd boldnes, my humility
In thanks declares yor bounty, as yo^{u} haue
Bene parent to my expectation
Giue heat to warme it & to keep it liuing. /
Con. To flatter yo^{u} were to desire yor ruine,
And to torment yo^{u} wth a sad discouragem^{t}
were to offend ag^{t} that virgin goodnes
I'm tender of & [I am] confidently think
you value highly.
Sp. Let the words I [vtter] speake
Infect the aire wherein I draw my breath
wth more abhorrid vapor then the smoke
That fumes from *Ætna*, if my thoughtꝭ intend
Their satisfaction but in noble[n] wayes.
Ien. S^{r} my m^{r} gaue me charge yo^{u} should not haue
So long an interview, & if yo^{u} will vndoe

911 /] positioned as in MS

me and my husband, & a whole housefull of
children, I vnderstand not how we shall be
recompenc't.

[FOL. 116 p. 12]

Sp. Beleeue ⌜it⌝ as I am a gentleman 116 12
I will not deale vnworthyly.
Ien. Nay then yo^{u} may goe a little further
For if yo^{u} can ꝓtest like a gentleman yo^{u}
are i the better case, & I the sooner dischar=
ged, & o my modesty S^{r} pay all & take all, I
am for turns at need, & though we cherish
the old yet we know o^{r} liuing must come
by the yong. *Enter Peter*
Pet. Wife my m^{r} mistrustꝭ you'l yeeld ⌜to⌝ that wch is
not fit for yo^{u} to yeeld‸ ⌜to⌝, & sent me to bid y^{u}o
be an honest woman & be carefull of his iew=
ell.
Sp. Is yor m^{r} at home S^{r}?
Pet. No S^{r} gone abroad vpon country busines
[but] ⌜and⌝ made me light of the gray gelding
to [say] ⌜deliu^{r}⌝ this [errand] ⌜message⌝ to my wife.
Sp. If you had spoken softly yo^{u} had shewed
more wit, but ꝓclaymeing yor [message] ⌜errand⌝
[like a ꝓclamation] alters the case, & so get
yo^{u} after him or Ile pink yor turky gro=
gram. ⌜*Drawes*⌝ *Exit Pet.*
Con. Do not yo^{r}selfe an iniury deare S^{r}
By being violent
Ien. Good m^{r} Spruse begone, the times yo^{u} see
are dangerous, scoutꝭ abroad not an ho=
nest woman but suspected, but it is euer
so, doe an old heauy vnwieldy Iustice a
kindnes & heel cry woman I know yo^{u} not
& then are we faine to cry a plague of him
y^{t} rode oth' black horse pay o^{r} fees & trade‸ ⌜afresh⌝
tis a fine world when the m^{r} of [th']‸ ⌜a⌝ compa=
ny will reueale the secret of a trade.

937 *y^{u}o*] *u* pushed back due to lack of space   948 *Drawes*] interlineation written across box marking stage direction

Con. Sweet S^{r} be pleasd to take the councell she
Giues yo^{u} I dare say for yor own behoofe
A parting freind wth feruency expectꝭ
His friends^ ⸢return⸣, this hath not bene the first

[Fol. 116v p. 12v]

nor shall it wth heauens fauour be the last
day [we haue taken comfort in] ⸢of o^{r} [meeting] mutuall comfortꝭ⸣.
Ien. [Good S^{r}]
Ien. Giue me an earnest yo^{u} affect my m^{ris}
And Ile indeauour any thing but being
Disloyall to her, if the old man mistrust
Ile giue him cause. ⌊*Giues her gold.*
Sp: This is ye midwife to all vndertakeingꝭ
Let it be dainty handed now & I
Shall euer praise it.
Ien. Prayse at parting as yo^{u} find me trust
me. Im [sure]^ ⸢true⸣ as steele.
Sp. Be yo^{u} ꝑpitious too or I am curst
The minist^{r}ꝭ vnlock the temple dore
But from the Oracle comes ye benediction
For wch I kneele to yo^{u}.
Con [To pause & think] ⸢Rise gentle S^{r},⸣
[Vpon a ꝑposition is a step] [⸢Cleard from the danger of despaire,⸣]
[If it be good to gracious intertainm^{t}] ⸢Cheare vp yor selfe & shake of sad despaire⸣
[If bad to slight reiection, as I see cause] ⸢Perhaps this day may be the witnes of⸣
⸢more happines then a succeeding yeare⸣
[Ile doe, but hope the former.] ⌊*Ex: Con. & Ien.*
⸢We must expect not set a time to^ ⸢take⸣ [destinye]⸣
Sp. I ioy in this & on a setled groundwork
Fasten my hopes. I will not staine thy purenes
By repetition, but wth silent thinking
Honour thy goodnes & be dumb. Dick Crisp.
Cris. S^{r}? S^{r}?

976 *Sp.*] over *on* of smudged *Con* 980–6 *[To ... destinye]*⸣] Constance's speech originally read: *To pause & think | Vpon a ꝑposition is a step | If it be good to gracious intertainm^{t} | If bad to slight reiection, as I see cause | Ile doe, but hope the former.* It was finally revised to read: *Rise gentle S^{r}, | Cheare vp yor selfe & shake of sad despaire | Perhaps this day may be the witnes of | more happines then a succeeding yeare | We must expect not set a time to take.* The interlineation at 981, *Cleard ... despaire*, was cancelled in favour of *Cheare ... despaire.* 991 *S^{r}*] first *S^{r}* over illegible smudged word

Sp. Thou hast heard all?
Cris: most S^{r}.

not

Sp. Should the old iade be false now for I dare
mistrust the oth^{r}ꝭ purity.
Cris. If you'l take a fooles opinion S^{r} I [think] ⌜am ꝑswaded⌝
m^{ris} *Iennet* is but slippery ware to deale wth
yet I think S^{r} I can tell yo^{u} how she may
meet wth her mach.
Sp. Is thy genius so ready Dick?
Cris yes S^{r}.

[Fol. 117 p. 13]

117 13

Sp. Giue me thy meaneing.
Cris. S^{r} yo^{u} ꝑceaue she shewes an inclination to doe
yo^{u} seruice, she allmost confesseth her selfe as we
take her & wthout question is more plyant then
honest, & a man fitted would ouercome one‸⌜of her faculties⌝ sodain=
ly & make vse of the other‸⌜[wthout le] in a little time⌝, please you to leaue my
seruice to it selfe, & I will not misimploy it to
effect yor end.
Sp. Thanks thou [officious cutter of] ⌜officious [abridger] correcter⌝ of excrem^{t}ꝭ
Cris: Sr Ile not fayle I dare warrant yo^{u}, yo^{u} shall
iudge of the ꝓbabilitie of my ꝓposition & as
yo^{u} approue‸⌜it⌝ [Ile practise] let me goe on.
Sp. Offerd as I would wish, open the course yo^{u}
meane to run.
Cris. Then thus S^{r}.‸⌜m^{ris} Ienet⌝ for [yor] her own likelihood of gaine
[she] cannot when yo^{u} please‸⌜to desire it⌝ deny yo^{u} admission
[tance] ⌜though⌝ ꝑhaps she may diuers wayes restrayne
yor conference, but S^{r}‸⌜you⌝ once entred, & I wayting
on yo^{u}, Ile offer yo^{u} some of the confectionerꝭ
com̃odities wch yo^{u} may wth a large com̃endation
offer to yor m^{ris}, then I haueing certifyed to yo^{u} ⌜before⌝
S^{r} the priuy mark of some confetꝭ [bef] wch I will
haue made purposely of *Nux vomica* yo^{u} may
p^{r}sent them to m^{ris} *Iennet*, who haueing‸⌜bene⌝ euer

992 *hast*] terminal *t* over *h* 994 *not*] turned over line as in MS 1019 *admission*] *ssion* over *t=*

since she was thirteen both licorish & insatiable
will accept‸⌜them⌝ in hast eat‸⌜hem⌝ wthout further question
& immediatly fall down like‸⌜an astonisht⌝ [andrunken] crow
then may yo^{u} S^{r} [doe as yo^{u} please], haue a coach
ready away wth yor carriage, goe‸⌜to⌝ a place con=
uenient, & fitt yor [further] ⌜next⌝ actions to the
[next] ⌜further⌝ circumstances, & so yor humble seruant
S^{r}.
Sp. ⌜Ingenious Dick!⌝
The Enginers come short of thee in makeing
An apt contriuem^{t}, [a] ⌜great⌝ rewardꝭ [is] are due
To thy inuention, if the sequell be
Grac'd wth success, thy vigilance & care
[Shall thank] [thy [plot] [labour, & admire]] ⌜[plot,] [let o^{r} earnest heat]⌝
[moue‸ [⌜swiftly⌝] since great actions doe require]
[Celerity] Shall [know] ⌜feele⌝ thy m^{r} loues thee let o^{r} thoughtꝭ

[FOL. 117v p. 13v]

Shake of a slow pac'd negligence & be
Prompted to action by celeritye. *Exeunt.*

Fin: Act. 2.

Act. 3. Enter. [Crisp. &] m^{r} wild & Crisp.

Cris. As I am nimble fingerd‸⌜S^{r}⌝, & desire to be reputed to
haue a gracefull snap, my m^{r} values yo^{u} more
then any noble man in this kingdome.
wild. Ha's he not reason, did I euer borow mony of
him, to the poore ꝓportion of paying for my
going [at] ⌜in to⌝ a play, wth the noble excuse of a plague
o my page that carries my siluer‸⌜for staying so long⌝, when his
ho^{r} had not a cross about him, nor knew where to
get it?
Cris: yo^{u} S^{r}? no.
wild. Nor euer gracd him wth a curse of a pox on yo^{u} for
a rogue, when his Lop^{s} familiaritie was
onely ⌜vouchafd⌝ to get him‸⌜be⌝ bound wth him for mony.

1030 *andrunken*] first *n* squeezed between *a* and *drunken* 1031 ,] comma very faint 1038 *reward*ꝭ] ꝭ squeezed in 1041–3 *[Shall ... thought*ꝭ*]*⌝] probable order of revisions: *plot* cancelled in favour of *labour, & admire* immediately following; *labour, & admire* cancelled and *plot, let o^{r} earnest heat* interlined above; *Shall ... Celerity* cancelled in favour of *Shall ... thought*ꝭ at 1043 1041 *thy*] *y* over *e* 1053 *[at]* ⌜*in to*⌝] *in* and *to* are positioned above and on either side of *at*; *in at a play* may have been an intermediate reading revised to *in to a play* 1056 *get it?*] positioned, along with partial box, as in MS

Cris: These thingꝭ S^{r} are below yo^{u}

wild. Nether haue I offerd for his security my mano^{r}
of *Nullibi*, when S^{r} wiꝉꝉm Brocage the scriue=
ner can testify it was morgag'd to seuerall men
before, for he is a wittnes to the conueyances, &
his hand is at all the bookes.

Crisp: Farr be these poore thingꝭ from yo^{u} S^{r}.

wild. Then confess his estimation of me is vpon very
good grounds.

Cris: He acknowledgeth it be hind yor back S^{r}, wch is
the most [asu] infallible testimony.

wild. And I scorn [to be so base as] ⌜the basenes⌝ not to be reciprocall,
as I am now the top bow of a succession of two
& thirty descentꝭ I neuer was ignoble nor
could frame my selfe to be so.

Cris: Though yo^{u} are as great a gamster as any is
about town S^{r}, yet the very rookes ꝓtest yo^{u}
deale all vpon the square.

wild. Enuy cannot touch me wth the taxation of a buistle
die, a quicksiluerd bowle [n]or a smooth box yet I
know as much‸ ⌜as⌝ any of 'hem for [onely for to see]
[what oth^{r} men can doe,] I haue had my hand
tyed a night or two, to [see]‸ ⌜try⌝ if I could do it

[Fol. 118 p. 14]

14.

this way, & can at my plesure make one dy 118
sure out of a [ruffe]‸ ⌜scrued⌝ box, but [it was] onely to disco=
uer to my freinds, how some ill dispositiond fel=
lowes liue, I scorn the practise my selfe & ab=
horr the memory of so poore a designe. but enough
of this dick where doth thy m^{r} intreat my company.

Cris: He beseecheth yor stay here a small time‸ ⌜S^{r}⌝, & if he
come not wthin this q^{r} of an howre, hee'l wth the
speed. of conueniency wait vpon yo^{u} at yor chãber.

Enter Spruse.

But‸ ⌜he is⌝ here S^{r} allready.

1076 *great*] *r* over another letter, perhaps *e* 1083 *[see]‸*] caret positioned under terminal *e* 1085 118] folio number positioned in MS slightly under and between *make one* 1086 *[ruffe]‸*] caret positioned under *r*

Sp. Noble wild, the hast of my necessity con=
ceales a further exp^{r}ssion, but along wth me I
beseech thee.

wild. I wish the success may answer yor [vigilance] ⌜hast⌝. *Exeunt.*

*Enter M^{ris} mumble Sophia wth a maudlin
cup.*

mũ. Gone in hast sayst thou?

Sop. I forsooth.

mũ. Why forsooth, because I would know for=
sooth, may not I ask yo^{u} a question but yo^{u}
must ask me why forsooth, ha yo^{u} held vp a
countesses trayne so long & learnt no more
good maners?

Sop: I [to] answerd you dutyfully indeed forsooth.

mũ. mary did yo^{u} wth a small word I askt if yor bro=
ther were gone & yo^{u} sayd why forsooth.

Sop. Indeed mother I sayd I forsooth.

mũ. Nay then tis happy I mistooke no more my cup
wench & Ile drink to thee in forgiuenes.

Sop. Thank yo^{u}, forsooth. *She drinks all*

mũ. How should I ha done wth a great cup that
blow so wth drinking this little.

Sop. The cup's a prety draught forsooth,.

mũ. I wench we that are old must doe as we may
yet I ha known the day when I ha drunk three
of these of high country white [in] to my morning(
draught, & bene no fuller then needs must ne=
ther, & Ile tell thee the day too, it was the next
morning after thy father dyed, tis a [wofull] ⌜perills⌝ alter⟨ ⟩a

[FOL. 118v p. 14v]

tion for a woman[⟨ ⟩] to fall from three to one, & by
reason of her infirmityes to be stinted of her drink

Sop. you are not yet very weake.

mũ. I thats true I can speake or els fare well I,
but my dancing failes me, my drinking yo^{u} see
decayes, two Turkie eggs serue me now to
breakefast, when I haue heretofore eaten seuen

1124 *alter⟨ ⟩a*] blot obscures reading   1125 *woman[⟨ ⟩]*] letter hatched out; perhaps *t*

besides cold red deare & fryd clary, but thou
sayst right I can speake indeed.
Sop. I sayd yo^{u} were not very weake forsooth.
mũ. No? thou seest I goe wth a staffe.
Enter [a seruant.] ⌜*Godfrye.*⌝
Godf. Pray m^{ris} *Sophia* let my m^{ris} know here's m^{r}
Strife the Lawyer desires to see her.
mũ. How what sayes he; what sayes he?
Godf: m^{r} Strife the Lawyer is come to see yo^{u} forsooth.
mũ. Bid him come in Godfry bid him come in but∧ ⌜do not⌝
tell him I goe wth a staffe. *Sophia*, take my
staffe & those thing(away wth hem, thou knowest
his busines he's [like]∧ ⌜in election⌝ to be my second husband.
Sop. Is he so forsooth?
mũ. Let him goe forsooth? shall I [say so] ⌜do so⌝ by yo^{u}, [must] ⌜would⌝
not euery thing liue, & must not yong tur=
kies [be fedd at their vsuall howres] ⌜haue their feeding⌝, let him
go quoth a? [O] Come come girle be not ag^{t}
thy moth^{r}, & thou shat ha the ƀre portion.
Sop. I hope youl be as good as yor word forsooth.
mũ. mary will I girle, thy napkin me thinks my
nose drops & my lips are clam̃y. ⌊*She wipes.*
Now Lawyer I defy thee doe thy worst ⌊*sings.*
Enter Mr Strife, & a seruant.
A prety good treble still *Sophia*, prety
cleare prety cleare
Strife. I may wthout speakeing for fauour or affection,
[or f] [&] ⌜&⌝ wthout feare of haueing a writ of errour
brought ag^{t} my opinion conclude so too, wth yor
good leaue licence sufferance & ꝑmission I take
possession of the p^{r}misses. ⌊*Kisseth her.*
mũ. Saucy knaue away heare yor m^{ris} secret(. ⌊*Ex. Godfrye*
that she will impart to∧ ⌜none but⌝ her councell ⌊[*uant*]

1136 ⌜*Godfrye.*⌝] thin penstrokes with the word positioned slightly high on the line suggest this is a late revision 1137 *Godf.*] over *Ser.*; thin penstrokes suggest this revision made at the same time as the revision at 1136 and 1140 1140 *Godf:*] over *Ser.*; thin penstrokes suggest this revision made at the same time as the revision at 1136 and 1137 1146 ?] over comma; comma serves as point to question mark 1152 *thinks*] Osborne *s*? 1163 *Godfrye*] *Godf* over *Ser=* 1164 *[uant]*] second syllable of *Seruant* (cf. note to 1163)

119 15

Strife. And hopeth that he yor said [Thomas] [Strife] ⌜seruant⌝ shall quiet=ly hold occupie possess & inioy the same,

mũ. you are a very learned man m^{r} Strife.

Strife. And haue free ingress regress & egress.

mũ. yor deep words I vnderstand not.

Strife. wthout [a] ⌜any⌝ let hindrance molestacõn disturbance interruption or euiction whatsoeuer

Sop. As this depon^{t} veryly thinketh, as‸ ⌜was written in⌝ the paꝑ [told] [me] that lapt vp my tiffany, yo^{u} [owe] ⌜wooe⌝ like an Ass.

mũ. what sayes she m^{r} strife?

Strife. She sayes the Arcadia is a bett^{r} authour then [my] [Lo: Cookes] Littleton, & cõmends [m] *Sr Phil. Sidney* before my Lo. [Cooke.]‸ [⌜*Diar*⌝] *Diar.*

mum. Nay itꝭ a parills wench but let her alone age will reaue her m^{r} strife. yo^{u} must not be angry with her the wench wishes yo^{u} well but she will haue a gird sometimes at her best freinds, & mettle in a yong thing is worth cherishing that yo^{u} know as well as I.

Strife. Indeed I ha many times seene a wild yong man after a yeares swinge or two follow his study close & in conuenient time turn a good student I meane for a [s] chamber practiser.

mũ. Ha yo^{u} so? how sa?

Strife. Euen‸ ⌜so⌝ may m^{ris} *Sophia* in time.

Sop. Liue to see yo^{u} sell yor bookes, & turne a country Atturny.

Strife. A well wisher to yor mother deserues more respect in Law. Truly yor vsage is not good in Law.

Sop. yo^{u} will not haue me leaue yo^{u} forsooth?

mũ. As thou wilt *Sophia* I ha not had a quame a great while I would be loth to tell [my suiter] ⌜m^{r} Strife⌝ any ontroth or to cousin a gentleman wth a diseased body that comes to me in loue.

1166 *yor*] over *the*　　1178 *Sidney*] secretary *e*

Sop. Indeed. forsooth yor too forward. [*whisꝑs this & Exit.*
Strife Nor I^⌜you⌝ nor any^⌜gentle⌝ woman y^{t} would think me worthy [of] ⌜to⌝
be her husband. I lead the mesures euer next to
the iudges still ⌜on Allhollow day & candlemas⌝, was Prince once m^{r} oth' reuells
long, & haue yet a reputation, [w^{ch}] wthout fraud or co=
uen [I desire yo^{r}selfe] to [inquire of] ⌜goe very⌝ vpright

[FOL. 119v p. 15v]

mũ. And when a man is past forty & a woman thirty
they say they decline, [yet] ⌜but⌝ me thinks I am p^{r}ty vigo=
rous still, yet I ha past that age somwhat
Strife Lying alone do's yo^{u} much harme, it were farre more
vsefull behoouefull & aduantageous for yo^{u} to be vn=
der couert barne, the english of the french is to
be maried forthwth.
mũ. yo^{u} say very true m^{r} strife, for then all the care will
not lye vpon a body though much of the busines.
Strifo Then ꝓuided allwayes yor mind be so setled conueyed
& assured, as I hope yo^{u} haue no cause but to think
yor promise irreuocable. yo^{u} may haue yor husband
meaning my selfe to follow yor law busines wthout a
fee.
mum. I so I may.
Strife. I will direct yor seruantꝭ, & saue yo^{u} the expence of
meat drink & wages to an ouerseer, bayly or stuart,
mum. Reasonable well.
Strife I shall receaue yor rentꝭ for yo^{u} wthout putting yo^{u}
to the trouble of weighing ⌜y^{e}⌝ gold, or fouling yor fin=
gers wth counting yor siluer.
Mum. And then account to me for all yor receiptꝭ?
Strife. Then I shall be rather a seruant then a husband.
mum. How?
Strife. Then I shall not haue the reputation of a husband
but onely the toyle of a seruant.
mum. Why I hope [to] yo^{u} will not think much to doe
my [drudgery] ⌜busines⌝?
Strife. No good m^{ris} mumble, Ile make yor will when

1204 *the iudges*] '& hang⟨ ⟩' or perhaps 'change' written above in very faint ink and slightly smudged (the interlineation is barely visible) 1216 *Strifo*] *o* perhaps a poorly formed *e*

[yo^{u}] I see yo^{u} palpably decay, & all such thing(in ma=
ner & form followeing.

mum. Then you meane to outliue me.

Strife. Not I but I [deale] ⌜tell⌝ yo^{u} that it will be safe for yo^{u}
& for auoiding controuersies to make a deed [to]‸ ⌜of⌝
gift to me of all then yo^{u} may dye the quieter

mũ. Nay then farwell honest squire spruce of *Norfolk*
my first, & Thomas mumble of London m^{r}chant
my second husband, that would neuer tell me of
death for feare of breakeing my hart ⌜seldome comes a better⌝. [but]&I see
yo^{u} [gownemen] ⌜lawyers⌝ are all for [yo^{r}selues] w^{t} has she?

[FOL. 120 p. 16]

120 16

Strif. Mistake not yor councell pray forsooth, yo^{u} shall cõ=
mand all, & me yor husband wholy & soly for the said
terme if it shall so happen that yor said selfe shall liue
so long. els I [I] hope.

mũ. Els I hope! Come come S^{r} since yo^{u} came to me as a
suiter, Ile [⟨ ⟩e] bring‸ ⌜you⌝ out [wi] ⌜in⌝ courtesie, & so bid yo^{u} fare=
well but indeed your too couetous to mary a gentle=
woman of good fashion‸ ⌜all for yo^{r}selfe, fy⌝. A cup of voiding beare
for m^{r} strife, a cup of voiding beare for the gentle=
man. *Exeunt Strife. & m^{ri}(mumble.*

Enter Spruse leading m^{ris} Constance by the arme.
m^{r} wild & M^{ris} Iennet. Crisp & Iony.

Iony. Mr Spruse I wonder you's take away my master you's
make him lewse the fairest match that euer had man
the deels ha me S^{r}, tis vara weel if a yong neg
get his charges the first yeare of his trening.

wild Hold yor tong yo^{u} ass & stay at the dore till I come to
thee so vnmanerly to press in where gentlewomen
are!

Iony. Why pre s^{r} are not all horsemen gentlemen, I haue
heard of a Lady has done penance for lying wth a [g] ⌜coach⌝=
man, & then tis no hurt for [hum]‸ ⌜gentlewomen⌝ ta luke vpon a horse

1240 *[to]‸*] caret positioned under *t*
1245 *[but]&I*] & squeezed in
1253 *[⟨ ⟩e]*] obscured letter perhaps *t*
1268 ⌜*coach*⌝=] hyphen not interlined
1269 *[hum]‸*] caret positioned under *m*

man. I [am] ⌜s⌝ sure S^{r} horsemen oft get mere then their mast^{r}ꝭ & though seldome a Iockie turne Lerd, yet a Lerd will often times turn a Iockie, [& be a higher man then] [too then whan he is a]

wild. Get the articles ready & I will [p^{r}sently] set my hand to [it] hem p^{r}sently.

Iony. Nay S^{r} then an you's not be councelld by yor horseman pray take ya^{r} neg to th' high way, an ya wi not be ruld, a horseman can neuer get credit by seruing sike a m^{r}, pre S^{r} gang, the scriuenersat the dore, & yor adu^{r}sary has set his hand to all reedy, & I's sure tis the fairest set that euer was ridden. [&]^⌜Oh⌝ y^{t} *I* were weight Is in a feare you's leust wth rading.

wild. Kit Spruse I onely take the liberty to article for a horsematch, yor occasions shall not want me before my return tender yo^{u}^ ⌜my presence⌝ & yor Lady my seruice.

Spr: yo^{u} know the appointm^{t}, & I hope will be mindfull how necessity calls for dispatch.

wild I will not neglect thee for a world, I can dispatch in an instant. *Ex wild & Iony.*

Spr. In the progress of my life, no [infelicity] ⌜occurrence⌝ hath made
⌜accident forcd me⌝
me so sensible of torm^{t}, nor [giue in me occasion] to account my selfe vn[happy] ⌜fortunate⌝, as the want of y^{t} felicitie wch yor

[Fol. 120v p. 16v]

absence occasioneth.

Con. If success be answereable to the desires of some of yor well wishers, yo^{u} will not long suffer vnder the burthen of [such] ⌜so great⌝ a vexation.

Sp: Wth yor own fauour & the connieueance of yor good freind m^{ris} *Iennet*, I shall p^{r}sume to make my visi= tations more frequent

Ien. S^{r} I was euer a freind to mery meetingꝭ, yet I can assure yo^{u} S^{r} ouer & besides, I neuer did a kindnes but the partie gaue me thanks

Sp. mine app^{r}hension makes me vnderstand I owe yo^{u}^ ⌜much,⌝, the [raine] ⌜aire⌝ doth please to [yeeld] giue

1270 *I [am]* ⌜*s*⌝] revised version reads *Is* (i.e., contracted form of *I is*) 1277 *horseman*] *a* over *e* 1278 *scriuenersat*] *s* squeezed between *scriuener* and *at* 1280 *[&]*^] caret positioned under *&* 1284 *yo^{u}*^] caret positioned under *u* 1304 *yo^{u}*^] caret positioned under *u* ⌜*much,*⌝,] duplication of punctuation as in MS

Showres to‸ ⌜the⌝ earth, that by that [moyst]‸ ⌜sweet⌝ refreshing
It may haue an abilitye to yeeld.
Both hearbs for [health] ⌜smell⌝, & [plesu] flowers for delight
To make the region healthfull: And I know
Though yo^{u} expect not yet Im bound to giue
Thanks in a full ꝓportion; this ring
Perhaps will fit yor finger, but my mind
Intends a larger recompence wch I
Promise & owe;; & if you'l ioyne wth me
To beg my pardon of yor gracious m^{ris}
That I forbeare in some rich p^{r}sentation
To let my seruice ho^{r} her, she shall
Appoint the form the matter & the [worth] value
Sheel haue me doe her homage in, & [beare] ⌜yo^{u}⌝
[wth this] Engage yor freind that by yor [obsecration]‸ ⌜mediation⌝
I am freed from guilt of a delinquencie.

Con. Those com̃on wayes of seruice are requir'd
Where the man wantꝭ ꝑfection, & giftꝭ
Are more sukcessfull wth the chambermaid
Then p^{r}ualent wth women of desert

Sp: [Height of‸ desert] ⌜An eminence⌝ liues in yor [high]‸ ⌜braue⌝ discerne
W^{ch} I must reuerence,

Ien. m^{r} Spruse me thinks
you haue bene a prety time here, will yo^{u} not
Wthdraw a while vntill we do inquire
wheth^{r} my m^{r} be returnd or no; some country
people that were at the meeting
Say he will be at home [incontinently] ⌜forth wth⌝.

Sp. Sweet m^{ris} *Iennet* be not so vnkind
To him y^{t} is yor freind yor thankfull freind
No such mistrust liues in yor vertuous m^{ris}
yet her it most concerns. *Enter wild.*

wild. I haue not much outstaid yor expectation
Pardon my rudenes Lady, tis a good iest
To see how fellowes liue about the towne

1305 *[moyst]*‸] caret positioned under *o* 1312 *larger*] *l* over *t* 1313 *owe;;*] duplication of punctuation as in MS 1314 *gracious*] *g* over another indiscernible letter 1319 *[obsecration]*‸] caret positioned under *a* 1325 *of*‸] caret positioned under *o* *desert*] *t* over blotted *ue* *[high]*‸] caret positioned under terminal *h*

To foole away their mony.

Sp. Why prethee why?

[Fol. 121 p. 17]

121 17

wild. I ha made a match wth a yong fellow pox ont I ha for=
got his name, (but it(no matter he's an Ins of court(
⌜pceaue by his makeing maches⌝
man as yo^{u} may [see by his makeing maches],) that has
giuen me a stone ods of weight & yet his horse is lower
∧ ⌜then mine⌝ by two fingers, tis pity yong fellowes should liue about
town wthout some men of discern to keep hem company.

Con. When is't to be run S^{r}?

wild. Nay Lady there's the iest, he [so] would not by any
meanes yeeld to haue it run till the beginning of
Aprill, because he should want mony till his Ladie dayes
rent came in; [because]∧ ⌜for⌝ he said it was ignoble to run & not stake.

Con: Alas good gentleman.

wild. And for all this he would needs pay the reckning, &
chang'd an Elizabeth angell to doe it wch he said his mo=
ther gaue him when he was a child, here are the re=
mainder of the sweet meates will yo^{u} tast. *He giues thẽ they tast.*

Sp. I am the least beholding to my memory of any
man liuing, Dick the boxe I gaue yo^{u}.

Cris: Those the musk, those the pearle & those the amber,
S^{r}.

Ien. The amber confet(are good restorers pray giue me
them. *He giues her confets*

Con. There's no comparison m^{r} Wild betwixt yor [⟨ ⟩]confect(
& m^{r} Spruse his,.

wild But to come as they did there lyes the iest, this
yong fellow now's a p^{r}ty whelp for me to enter.

Con. Where run yo^{u} S^{r} pray?

wild. But at Hide park Lady. Twill be a good recrea=
tion in an Euening for yo^{u} to giue vs the looking
on.

1354 *[because]*∧] caret positioned under *a* 1367 *[⟨ ⟩]*]reading uncertain; perhaps *8*

Sp. By that time my new coach will be finisht, & yo^{u}
shall ha the maidenhead of it, it wantꝭ nothing but
gilding of the arms behind, & vpon the p^{r}sumpti=
on of my hopes ꝓbability, I haue taken the bold=
nes to put in one [q^{r}] coate more then euer [of] o^{r} fa=
mily quarterd, w^{ch} [when yo^{u} behold will] p^{r}sumeꝭ
to call yo^{u} m^{ris}.
Ien. O the megram. the megram,
wild. Pox the woodeuill is it not, the old beast hath
the gidd. *Iennet turns round & falls downe.*
Con. O what ailes the woman?
Sp. No harme deare m^{ris}.
wild. A little drunk nothing els.
Sp. Ile tell yo^{u} truth
That I might haue a free fruition

[Fol. 121v p. 17v]

Of yor deare p^{r}sence, my seruant skill'd in simples
Did make these confectꝭ, wch will stupefy
And numm the sences that the party greeu'd
Will ly a time in such a strange distraction
As she appeares; yet yo^{u} need not feare, these partitions
directed [me] wch were
for her
Con. And^ ⌜will she⌝ take no hurt by being so?
Cris: No hurt at all, tis nux vomica
A simple wch they vse to catch crowes wth.
wild. Alas good buzzard. what a [scuruy] [thing] ⌜beastly sight⌝ is
a [drunken] woman [to looke vpon.] drunke!
Sp. As yo^{u} haue granted many [gracious] ⌜humble⌝ suits
To me yor seruant, so vouchafe me fauour
Once more, & that will make amends for all
The sufferingꝭ I haue born [wth patience.] ⌜vnwillingly.⌝
Daigne me yor p^{r}sence in some other place
Then this wch yo^{u} know is so liable
To danger that we cannot whisper safely.
Ile take of all the doubtꝭ yo^{u} can oppose
By a kind of anticipation
you can not blame [n]or [doubt] ⌜question⌝. this gentleman

1395–6 *directed . . . her*] squeezed into space after Constance's line   1409 *anticipation*] second *a* over *i*

Shall be companion of my seruice till
you be ꝑswaded no close priuacy
Can do yor honour iniury. Consider
How yor assent may giue extremitie
Of happines to him that honours you
Beyond [an] [⌜the⌝] [app^{r}hension or] expression
[Of a man mortall.] If disloyalltie
Or tender of my satisfaction
Aboue yor high prizd dignitie [haue]‸ ⌜had⌝ place
In these obseruant thoughtꝭ to yor indearem^{t}
Iustice would not haue giuen me liberty
To [such a dissentany] ⌜haue made a feyned⌝ ꝓtestation
But [giuen] ⌜sent⌝ reward to falsehood in a trice
Wth death & vengeance.
Con you haue taken of
The colour of an opposition
you did not explicate yor own affection
But wth a sodaine earnest zeale you stroue
To [second] set a higher estimate vpon
my reputation then yor own delightꝭ.
Such a thing as mistrust Im not acquainted wth
The company forbids, the qualitie
Of ꝑsons ꝓmise greater faithfullnes
To wch I giue a firme credulitie
Of being nobly vsd.
wild. your now set free
Wthout the reach of an old midwifes eye
At least [as bad]‸ ⌜a⌝ woman of more frequent [practise] ⌜trading⌝
[Fol. 122 p. 18]
Cris: She hath some symptomes of recouery ⌞*She stirs.*
Sp. [As] ⌜Let⌝ yor deare mercy take compassion 122 18
Vpon the man whom neuer any influence
Of starrs [inspir'd] ⌜inioynd⌝ till now to be affected
Wth [adoration]‸ ⌜admiration⌝ of a womans maiestie
The time giues licence, opportunitie
Stands [wth a free] ⌜as⌝ I haue implord this gentleman

1413 *yor*] *r* over superscript *u* 1415 *you*] *u* very slightly raised 1419 *[haue]‸*] caret positioned under *e*
1422 *dissentany*]] hatched out 1434 *credulitie*] *l* over *t* 1440 *yor*] *y* over *d*

The witnes of the seruice I shall striue
To make a tender of. A coach at dore
[Stands]∧ ⌜Waits⌝ to receaue yo^{u} & a noble freind
Of mine will giue yo^{u} hospitable wellcome
Not as yo^{u} merit but as he is able.
The place some few miles distant, & the passage
As free from danger as the m^{r}chantꝭ wish
The way to th' Indies. please yo^{u} set one foot forward
Till yo^{u}∧ [⌜shall⌝] [please] ⌜ꝑmit⌝ Ile take no more vpon me
Then to sustaine this arme

Con: So great an earnestnes
[Secure] I [neuer saw till now] ⌜neuer could perceaue⌝ to liue in man
Accompanied wth lookes of care & loue.
Ile onely take the ꝓpositions
Into my thoughtꝭ to ruminate vpon
wch leaue me at free libertye & [leaue] ⌜offer⌝
The rest to faire success.

Sp. your not more free
Then you shall euer∧ ⌜be⌝ the liberty
I wish is onely to be bound to yo^{u}
But that I craue forgiuenes for expressing
Before you gaue me warrant. let my request
Now made at once for all petition yo^{u}
To take the coach wth speed. *Iennet rises & falls downe againe.*

Cris: She rises S^{r}

Sp: Hast as yo^{u} loue my being.

wild The more yo^{u} stay your in the greater danger
Of being surpris'd the amazed crow recouers.

Con. Then when you will goe on, ꝓpitious starrs
[Starrs &]∧ ⌜And⌝ you defend me.

Sp. [Th] my seruice & that wish
Shall keepe yo^{u} safe. *Ex: ōes pret: Iennet.*

Ien. Tis three howres since I drunk
the muscadine, theres no remedy *She rises & staggers & falls down againe.*

1448 *[Stands]∧*] caret positioned under *n* 1454 *yo^{u}∧*] caret positioned under *u* *[⌜shall⌝] [please] ⌜ꝑmit⌝*] *shall* interlined with caret above cancelled *please* then hatched out, and *ꝑmit* interlined beside cancelled *shall*; slight chance *shall ꝑmit* interlined as revision to *please* and subsequently altered, but position of caret before *please* and MS spacing of interlined words suggests *shall* and *ꝑmit* introduced as separate revisions 1473 *surpris'd*] first *r* over long *s* 1476 *[Th]*] *h* only partly formed

the tother nap will doe it. *Offers to rise. falls againe she sleeps*
It will not doe man or woman must yeeld
to their betters; muscadine & tostꝭ I subscribe
Enter Iustice Thrifty & Peter Parchm^{t}.

[Fol. 122v p. 18v]

Thrif: Peter
Pet. S^{r}.
Thrif: Thy getꝭ knaue thy getꝭ.
Pet. O I beseech yo^{u} S^{r}.
Thrif: Nay hide not from yor m^{r} S^{r}, tis no shame to haue
a reuenue by seruing a Iustice of peace.
Pet. True S^{r} such a one as yor worp O S^{r}.
Thrif: What S^{r}.
Pet: My ostentation is fitter in anoth^{r} place S^{r}, for to tell
you the truth‸⌜what⌝ I haue heard abroad, could not but
make yor worp blush, [to heare]‸⌜at the vnfolding⌝ yor own abilities [vn=]
[folded.]
Thrif: As I told yo^{u} peter It would make a man of ꝑtꝭ
forsweare the bench to heare the [poore‸ fellowes] ⌜inferiour Iustices take so⌝
‸⌜like simplicians⌝ call the baylifes oth' hundred knaues, & threaten
a fine for want of attendance.
Pet. Tis very true S^{r} how imꝑtinently yor next neigh=
bour I meane othe left hand interrupted yor wor^{p}
[when] in yor discourse of the necessity of alehouses
& [yo] ye modern abuse of 'hem, & then fell of wth
a cry yo^{u} mercy S^{r} truly I mistooke yo^{u}.
Thrif: I tell thee Peter as I told thee before, there is
not one in a whole apparance at a sessions, y^{t}
knows how to distinguish busines or to set proceedingꝭ
in a method, & but that a man is bound by
the law of nature nations & [a] good conscience
not to hide his partꝭ when [⟨ ⟩] he may do good to
his country, [wth making vse of hem], I would
leaue the dull company of my fellow Iustices be=
cause they know not where lyes the center of a
busines, as I heard one say but he shall be name

1498 *poore‸*] caret positioned under *r* 1507 *sessions*] *e* has been adjusted; original reading unclear 1508 *knows how*] *s* squeezed in 1511 *[⟨ ⟩]* reading unclear; perhaps *O*

les because it is not fitt the weakenes of
authoritye should by an vnaduised disclosure of
him that [should] ⌜is trusted &⌝ ought to keep councell render a
magestrate contemptible, what dost thou think
I heard him say!

Pet. O S^{r} I dare not guess.

Thrif: Peter as I told thee he being‸ ⌜wide of y^{e} matter controu^{r}ted⌝ at least [wide] the
whole extent of a township, [of the matter contro=]
[uerted], was vrgd by the more discreet & men ƀre
qualified to speake ad rem, he answerd if [he] I do
not Ile speake to the purpose, now [didst] dost not
thou think this fellow handled his matters poorely

[FOL. 123 p. 19]

123 19

to make himselfe‸ ⌜so⌝ ridicalous in the face of his country

Pet: wonderfull weakely wthout doubt S^{r}.

⌜some of these men p^{r}sumd to question⌝

Thrif Nay Peter as I told thee before, my sufficiency [was]
⌜wch 8 Lo cheefe Iustices haue approud⌝
[questiond] [but it was by the malicious], & the offence
they tooke was I could speake latin [& vsd it] ⌜& not they⌝. Come come
times are worse & worse, a rich tradesman is made a
[⌜now y^{u} vnderstandst me⌝] ⌜& then is busines swayed as⌝
Iustice, a man of quality put out. [if the Iudges clerk]

[X] [oth' fines take a displesure ag^{t} a man, yo^{u} must giue]
[him a good breakefast, or yor credit is irreparable] ⌜he pleases,⌝
[⌜of [ye mano^{r}⌝] [⌜hard⌝]] ⌜hard⌝
[wth his Lo,:]‸ & tis [heard]‸ that a fellow of no greater
desert should ꝓcure a repriue before a noblemans

1516 *weakenes*] round terminal *s* over *sses* 1532–5 *Nay . . . not they*⌝] the original reading, *Nay Peter as I told thee before, my sufficiency was | questiond but it was by the malicious, & the offence | they tooke was I could speake latin & vsd it*, was revised to, *Nay Peter as I told thee before, some of these men p^{r}sumd to question my sufficiency | wch 8 Lo cheefe Iustices haue approud & the offence | they tooke was I could speake latin & not they* 1533 *8*] reading uncertain 1535–40 *Come . . . pleases,*⌝] the original reading, *Come come | times are worse & worse, a rich tradesman is made a | Iustice, a man of quality put out. if the Iudges clerk | oth' fines take a displesure ag^{t} a man, yo^{u} must giue | him a good breakefast, or yor credit is irreparable*, was revised to, *Come come | times are worse & worse, a rich tradesman is made a | Iustice, a man of quality put out. & then is busines swayed as | he pleases,*. The phrase *now y^{u} vnderstandst me* was interlined for insertion after *Iustice* (1538), then cancelled; ⌜*he pleases,*⌝ (1540) interlined above *him . . . breakefast* 1539–41 *[X]*] pencilled *X* hatched over in ink 1541 *[⌜of [ye mano^{r}⌝] [⌜hard⌝]]* order of revisions: *of ye mano^{r}* interlined with caret and *ye mano^{r}* subsequently cancelled; *hard* inserted and cancelled; a third single penstroke then crosses out *of . . . hard*; *hard* interlined a second time with caret 1542 *Lo,:]*‸] caret positioned under colon *greater*] *gr* over two other letters; second letter probably *e*

ŧre yet these are burdens, wch a shoulder vnaccusto=
md would be sore to support, but the vulgar thankfully
⌜at not being sensible of⌝
smile [at] their own oppressions.

Iennet rises & coms toward them ree= ling.

Pet. my wife come to bid yor worꝑ well come home.

Thrif: Housekeeꝑ. how fares all w^{th}in? did yo^{u} obserue re=
member & execute?

Ien. Thingꝭ go not so well as they should forsooth

Pet. Thatꝭ true for thou goest as if $[y^{u}]$∧⌜thou⌝ wert drunk
go so well as they should, why thou canst not
stand; as I am vertuous S^{r} she's drunk. ⌜pfectly⌝

Thrif: Fy fy say not so. say not so. ⌜drunk an like⌝ ⌜ye.⌝

Pet. Thingꝭ goe not so well as they should; quotha,
they go ill fauourdly for thou reelst euery step,
indeed wife thingꝭ go not so well as they should
I am of yor mind wife, tis granted they doe not.

Ien. I beseech yo^{u} S^{r} hearken to y^{e} suit of an∧⌜vnwilling⌝ $offendo^{r}$
& because I will not [offend] ⌜trouble⌝ yo^{u} wth tediousnes re=
ceaue y^{e} worst first & if my death satisfy, I con=
fess I haue my reward though yo^{u} not yor child.

Thrif: How?

Ien. S^{r} I was made drunk, & till iust now∧⌜did not⌝ recouer[d]
& they y^{t} did this villany stole away my yong
m^{ris} I confess S^{r}, I confess; but cannot help it.

Thrif: Why, Peter. *He chafes & turns about*

Pet. Here S^{r}.

Thrif: Peter I say. as I told yo^{u} before, Peter I say.

Pet. At yor wor^{ps} elbow S^{r},

Thrif. O Peter thy wife is a thing, that is not worthy of
my fury, though heretofore she hath alayed my heat.

Pet. S^{r}. [N]

Thrif. Nay since she is as she is Ile tell thee what she
has bene, & all her faultꝭ shall receaue a condigne
$punishm^{t}$ $togeth^{r}$.

1550 ?] over comma; comma serves as point to question mark   1553 *[y^{u}]∧*] caret positioned under colon   1555–7 *pfectly . . . ye*] tighter lettering and fainter ink suggests this is a late revision; last two lines of passage squeezed into space provided by Thrifty's half-line   1555 *pfectly*] no abbreviation mark on *p*   1560 *wife*] minim before *w* crossed out   1579 *$punishm^{t}$ $togeth^{r}$*] positioned as in MS

but as I told yo^{u} before stole away dost thou say?
Ien. Too true I assure yor wor^{p}. *She kneeles.*
Thrif: A warrant for a priuy search Peter;, and then weel
inquire the names of the men that should be lookt
after.
Pet. Not to displease yor wor^{p}, I think their names
would [very]‸⌜more⌝ ꝓꝑly be known first, els yo^{u} giue di=
rection to looke yo^{u} know not whom.
Thrif: As I told yo^{u} before, passion transports me in the
course of‸⌜Iusticiary⌝ ꝓceedingꝭ, but thy memory inables thee
to be recorder of a town corporate, therefore take
Iennets examinacõn, & then draw the warrant.
Stand vp & pray for the bench when yo^{u} are acquited.
She stands vp & makes cursie.
Nay as I told yo^{u} before it was impossible she should
be true to her m^{r} y^{t} would cuckold her husband
when he was writing ith' next roome nay this I
know of mine own knowledge.
Peter. O goodnes defend S^{r}.
Thrif: As I told thee before Peter 'twas onely wth [thee] ⌜me⌝
& tis a grace for thy seale ring to haue bene
vpon thy m^{rs} finger, but no more of that now,
as I told thee before twas onely wth me, but
to giue thee satisfaction I bequeath thee this
Tufftaffata Ierkin, & wthout more expostulation
accept it as a wor^{p}full recompence. *Giues him a ierkin of his back*
Pet. I am content S^{r}, but [my] ⌜me⌝ thinks I feele
bunches rising here S^{r}. [I pray] ⌜I pray⌝ looke I think you
may see 'hem wthout spectacles. *He lookes of his forehead.*
Thrif: O my worpfull word the biting of
a gnat. But on to the examinacõn, now I must
lay [of] ⌜by⌝ my familiarity, & exercise [my] authority in
the seat of Iudicature. *He goes into ye chaire*
Woman woman how write you yor selfe?
Ien. An please yor wor^{p} ye right wor^{p}full Iustice Thriftyes
house keeꝑ.

1586 *[very]*‸] caret positioned under *ry*   1604 *Tufftaffata*] medial *t* over *f*

Thrif: That sounds scuruily & the cadence is incongr⌜u⌝ous
when by misdemeanours ill disposed people leaue
of to doe well, they loose the priuiledge, wch they
[m^{rs} fauour afforded them.] ⌜had by following those they belong'd to.⌝
Ien: Some fauour I beseech yo^{u} S^{r} for old loue.
Thrif: Woman I know thee not, Iustice is impartiall & ⌜must not⌝
[knowes not] ⌜take acquaintance of⌝ the face of an offendor, though she be
⌜Peter on to her examinacõn.⌝
a Lady of ꝑtꝭ, but [ill members of the com̃on wealth]
Woman woman, who ist yo^{u} suspect?
Ien. I ha three or fowre in suspition, S^{r} but yor wor^{p} gaue
me leaue to giue one more lib̄y then the rest, & so I

[Fol. 124 p. 20]

124 20

hope yo^{u} will therefore be‸ ⌜the⌝ more ready to forgiue.
Thrif: How ⟨ ⟩?
Ien. yes indeed S^{r}, for m^{r} Spruse did make a very gentle=
man like ꝓtestation, & I desir'd m^{ris} *Constance* to vse
him no otherwise then yor worpfull selfe had [com̃an=] ⌜directed⌝
⌜in case he did so⌝ [⌜w sometimes⌝]
[ded me to vse yor selfe] & I trust she did but [wheth^{r}]‸ ⌜whether⌝ wth
the drinking [my]‸ ⌜a great⌝ morningꝭ draught or eating some
confectꝭ m^{r} Spruse gaue me, I sounded & away they
went.
Thrif: Set down m^{r} Spruse [as] principall.
Pet: Tis done S^{r}.
Thrif: Who accessaries‸ ⌜assistantꝭ aiders or cõfort^{r}ꝭ.⌝ [now]; speake woman.
Ien: m^{r} wild forsooth, & *Crisp* m^{r} Spruces man.
Thrif: They may all go in a warrant Peter.
Pet: wonderfull well S^{r}.
Thrif: Ha yo^{u} put 'hem in?
Pet. yes S^{r}.
Thrif. The warrant must be ḡrall & so direct it.
Pet. Yo^{r} wor^{ps} hand an please yo^{u} S^{r}. *He sets his hand to.*
Ien. As I am modest S^{r} onely these were in fault, & I

1618 *wch they*] *y* over *ir* 1630 ⟨ ⟩] reading uncertain; looks like an *s* on its side topped with a superscript *r* 1633–5 *had ... selfe*] original reading is, *has commanded me to vse yor selfe*; *d* over *s* to alter *has* to *had*; *directed in case he did so* substituted in place of *commanded ... selfe*; *w* of *w sometimes* perhaps represents false start 1635 *[wheth^{r}]*‸] caret positioned under *he* 1640 *Pet:*] over *Ien.* 1642 ,] over full-stop 1644 *Pet:*] over *Ien.*

beseech yo^{u} consider it.

Thrif: Woman I tell thee as I told thee before, thy offence
is [great & vnheard of, & th] ⌜apparant⌝ & the eares of Iustice
must be deafe to the cries of the guilty.

Pet. One word for my wife S^{r} I beseech yor wor^{p}.

Thrif: Fellow fellow, as my Clerk I know thee but as one
y^{t} speakes for the delinquent thy face [is vnknowne] ⌜I am vnacquainted wth⌝
[to me], her fault ⌜is⌝ wthout p^{r}sident, & she must be punisht
accordingly, fy∧ ⌜a dry nurse⌝ be drunke when she should looke to her
charge. [I will repeat a little story & compare the caseꝭ]

Ien. S^{r} I was ou^{r}come by vnlawfull meanes.

Thrif: ∧ ⌜I,⌝ [So cry]∧ ⌜I, so crye⌝ all yor women offendo^{r}ꝭ, in truth it was my hard
chance to be ou^{r}come. thy fault is wthout example, & y^{u}
shalt haue a punishm^{t} of mine own deuise, to see the ig=
norance of o^{r} forefath^{r}ꝭ, that knew not how to fit [a puo] [⌜re=⌝]
a mulct to an affence, how im℘ꝑly haue they set women
behind y^{e} cart, & then whipd [vn] ⌜'hem⌝ inhumanely, I will ther
fore alt^{r} the practise, bate the whipping, haue thee &∧ ⌜thy⌝ [y^{r}]
confederates if they may be come by, draw a cart along
the streetꝭ, vpon a solemn day, & this is yor iudgem^{t}.

Ien. Good S^{r}. [take her away.]

Thrifty. Take her away, [for [⌜my⌝] clemency'sabusd too great] ⌜sententiously rebuk't⌝
[Is onely cur'd by being rigorous]
[A frequent mildnes makes offendo^{r}ꝭ insolent]
[And tis not [Iustice] [⌜mercy⌝] but a foolish pitye]
[[⌜giues conniuance to⌝][⌜men in⌝]]
[That [fauours any] [gross]∧ delinquencie [*Exeunt*]]
When those are spard should be seuerely vsd
mercy mistakes & Iustice is abusd. *Exeunt.*

Fin: Act. 3.

1652 ⌜*apparant*⌝] positioned above *great &* 1665 *women*] e over *a* 1671–6 *Take ... Exeunt*] passage apparently first read: *Take her away, for clemency abusd | Is onely cur'd by being rigorous | A frequent mildnes makes offendo^{r}ꝭ insolent | And tis not Iustice but a foolish pitye | That fauours any gross delinquencie.* Then *mercy* interlined above cancelled *Iustice*, and *men in* interlined above cancelled *gross*; *fauours any* and interlined *men in* then cancelled, and *giues conniuance to* interlined with caret, partly over top of *men in. Is onely ... Exeunt* then cancelled with diagonal hatchings, and opening line reworked as *my clemency's abusd too great* (*my* interlined above cancelled *for* and *'s* squeezed between *clemency* and *abusd*), before this phrase cancelled. Final reading is *Take her away, sententiously rebuk't.* 1677–8 *When ... Exeunt.*] over uncancelled act break which reads: *Fin. Act. 3...* 1679 *Fin: Act. 3.*] squeezed onto bottom of page

[FOL. 124v p. 20v]

Act 4.
Enter M^{r} wild & m^{ris} Sophia.

wild. If wthout screwing yor face into a posture of dislike or an
hipocriticall refuseing the affection of a man [resolud] ⌜of resolue⌝
(when I know it is most competible to yor sex though
⌜rath^{r} to accept then to cry I heare you not)⌝
a thing not so much worne)∧ you can comply wth a ꝓpo=
sition of one that neuer affected complem^{t}, & knowes
it is fantastick to vse ['hem] ⌜it⌝, I shall be ready to very⌜fy⌝ the
ꝓuerb, by shortning the course of sollicitation wth [a] ⌜a⌝
speedy closeing vp the match, & tyeing the knot [in=
dissoluble by any thing but death.]

Sop: Once I confess I saw yo^{u} when my broth^{r}
Gladly inioyd yor company, & brought
yo^{u} to my moth^{r}ꝭ house, where that poore pittance
wch p^{r}paracõn had made ready for
Her selfe & vs two yo^{u} in courtesy
pleasd [Seem'd] to accept, but had not a suspicõn
you app^{r}hended any worthines
In me to vrge ⌜you⌝ to this ꝓposition.

wild. Can yo^{u} receaue a more firme assurance
Then mine own ꝓtestation vnconstraynd.
[Then a] Conceipt first tooke me∧ ⌜then⌝, wch I [felt] confess
, , was worth the makeing much of, time the moth^{r}
, , Of truth did feed it, I ꝑceau'd it crescent
And pleasd in [each] ⌜the particular⌝ degrees[of augmentation]
Of augmentation was sincerely vrg'd
By the deuotion of yor [seruant w^{ch}] ⌜admirer⌝ which
Inhabitꝭ here, to giue it vtterance
In seruiceable words.

Sop: And I accept it
In a degree of thankfullnes, but dare not
[Afford it nearer wellcome] ⌜Restraynd by filiall obligation⌝
Afford it nearer wellcome.

wild. I cry yo^{u} mercy
my honourd peece of feminine modesty.

1702 *Conceipt*] *C* over *c*   1705 *degrees[of]* cramped spacing suggests *s* added late

I'm blunt, [&]‸⌜yet⌝ loue yo^{u}, & if yo^{u} be angry
perhaps there is ability in man
To cure that [*atra‸ bilis*] ⌜[⟨ ⟩] *atra bilis*⌝. giue me leaue
To tell yo^{u}, there was one yo^{u} know sollicited
In ho^{tt} forme, as I do yo^{u}; she pleasd
As the story will inform yo^{u} wth variety
At least, wth hope of change, refusd the offer[s]
Alleadg'd dislikeing parentꝭ did ꝑhibit
The gentlemans request, he being denyd
In time receded, as all men must doe
One time or other; but my virgin peece
(A time so but not long,) did catch a clap
And was constraynd by harsh necessity
Or the hard fortune of a brittle memory
wch could not name the father of the child
To lay't vpon | a seruing man, her parentꝭ
Greeud wth this sad disaster, askt the wench

[Fol. 125 p. 21]

why she did not rather mary then abuse   125   21
Her selfe & kinred she replyd she durst not
yet durst be got wth child wthout their licence
By a butler a meere trencher scraper. I
haue told the tale, & the wisest kingꝭ do imitate
[⌜euen⌝] [⌜the imitation⌝]
A game at Chess [eu'n] [in a battle royall] [the disposition]
[Of] [despicable pawnes] the despicable men
Being of no vse but to emblematise
—{ [The emperour of *Rome* did teach his seruant]
[His mind by cutting of the tops of bentꝭ.]
If yo^{u} can make example an instruction
you app^{r}hend & put in practise wisely.

Sop. If yo^{u} require a sodaine answer S^{r}
Ile hazard yor displesure I assure yo^{u}.

wild. As I would wish, thy first born child shall be
my eldest son. [I take that for granted.] ⌜Or els Ile want my⌝ will

1718 *atra‸*] caret positioned under *ra* ⟨ ⟩] single letter hatched out and illegible 1731 |] vertical bar positioned as in MS; perhaps cancels a small mark 1738–9 [⌜*the* ... *disposition*⌝]] order in which *the imitation* and *the disposition* introduced unclear 1739 *disposition*] *d* over *s* 1746 *require* ... *answer*] over smudged cancellation; original reading illegible 1749 *Or* ... *will*] *Or* ... *my* interlined above *I* ... *granted*; *will* positioned after *granted*

Sop. One of the two is like to come to pass.
But wch I will not say.
wild. Then open this
And if yo^{u} haue a competent ꝓportion
[To] Of loue to answer his y^{t} there salutes you.
I need no intercesso^{r}, if yo^{u} haue not
It is not the first [miserie my mind] ⌜but greatest miserie.⌝
[Hath bene tormented wth]. ⌜my mind hath bene acquainted wth.⌝

Enter M^{ris} mumble & Godfrye.

mũ. Is the gentleman come from my son.
Godf: yes [and gone in to] ⌜I left him wth⌝ my yong m^{ris}, they are both yonder forsooth.
mum. Intreat him to come nearer *Godfry*, I cannot speake loud.
Sop: The contentꝭ of this inioyne[s] me to giue an answer
wch my mothers so sodaine coming will at this time
restrayne me [to‸ satisfy yo^{u} wth] ⌜from [satisfying]⌝, but I hope yor [patience]
[will] acceptation will intertaine it another time.
wild. So much life in so little, will make [that wch followes.]
[more wellcome.] expectation vnweariedly attend.
Godf: Ant please yo^{u} S^{r} my old m^{ris} refresht wth the ioyfull ti=
dingꝭ yo^{u} are the bearer of, desires yor relation in ꝓ=
per ꝑson may satisfy her worP^{s} longing.
wild. I come to her freind p^{r}sently. *Godfrye goes back to‸ ⌜his⌝ m^{ris}.*
Then Lady let my ꝓbabilities
grow as I wish yor happines, & heark yo^{u}. *He whisꝑs her*
mũ. Did yo^{u} tell‸ ⌜him⌝ *Godfry*?
Godfr: yes forsooth.
mũ. Ha.
Godf: yes ant like yo^{u}.
mũ. That who would speake wth him?
Godf: [Had I no name.] you for sooth. | *mũ.* Had I no name.
God⌝ [*mum*] Forsooth I sayd my old m^{ris}es woP. didst y^{u} say to him yo^{u} forsooth.

1766 *to*‸] caret positioned under *to* ⌜*from [satisfying]*⌝] positioned with caret above *to* ... *wth* 1780–6 *That* ... *too*] probable process of revision: *Had I no name* | *Forsooth I sayd my old m^{ris}es woP* | *Out rascall* ... (1781–3) written; *Had* ... *name* cancelled and short reply by Godfrey (*you for sooth*) fitted in after; Mumble's next speech fitted into space at right of page over three lines and set off with partial box (1781–3). It seems likely that speech prefixes were added after these revisions made, and that *mum* (1782) and *Godf:* (1784) were inserted in error and subsequently corrected deep in left margin

⌜*Mum*⌝ [*Godf:*] Out rascall ou^{r}throw the likelihood of ꝓpagation, tmay
be tis an oth^{r} suiter, & if thou call me old ꝑhaps heel
mistake & think me so too

[FOL. 125V p. 21V]

Godf: THe ⌜gentleman⌝ can see forsooth.
mũ. But *Godfry* Loue is often blind oth' mans side, [but]
kiss yor hand & vsher me, the gentleman steps toward
vs. I beat a dog that offended me, & forgot to lay
by the staffe. ⌊*Throwes away her staffe*
wild. yor deseruing son, & my freind that I am happy in
being known to ⌜in these lines⌝ offers yo^{u} his duty.
mum. How dos my son S^{r} pray?
wild. Wonderfull well, & wantꝭ nothing but witnesses of
his good fortune he has had so faire a beginning
of his desires, that vnles [contradiction be an eni=]
[my to success, & his designes be a kin to the world]
[to haue feth^{r}ꝭ v⟨p⟩ run vp riuers, & squibꝭ leap ithe]
[faces of them that giue fire to hem, [I] barbers]
[haue their muschatoes turnd vp by their m^{rs}]
[& Iockies [ha] their stirrups held [vp] by their Lo:]
[men in authority make a retreat, & offendo^{r}ꝭ counte=]
[nance their‸ ⌜own⌝ artꝭ wth the face of resolution, a ram]
[kill a butcher, & brick battꝭ beat a hundred muske=]
[tiers] [&] pikes‸ [⌜& musketiers⌝], [more fields be made a bleching place]
[& fleet street a place [⌜platforme⌝] to exercise a company on]
[⌜noble⌝] [⌜gentle⌝ ⌜in his⌝]
[gownmen] [lead soldiers, & a [wiser]‸ man [then the]]
[⌜shirt⌝][⌜more acquainted⌝]
[generall come out in his, &.] [by the strength of]
[reason perswade them to be quiet. I say vnles some]
[of the most to be wondred at thingꝭ] [of these come]
[to pass, or a stranger then these giue him] some ⌜miraculous⌝ rub
of interruption ⌜cross him beyond likelihood⌝ he is a made man, & yo^{u} a moth^{r}

1799 *v⟨p⟩*] reading uncertain; only bowl of *p* formed 1804 ⌜*own*⌝] insertion not cancelled with rest of speech 1806 *pikes,*] not cancelled with rest of speech 1808–11 *[⌜noble⌝] ... his, &.*] original version: *& a wiser man then the generall come out in his, &. by the strength of reason perswade them to be quiet*; *wiser* first revised to *noble* and then to *gentle* (positioned with caret); phrase then partly developed to read *& a gentle man in his shirt more acquainted*. Revision seems abandoned thereafter, and whole passage was subsequently cut.

liuing till this age onely because yo^{u} brought
forth so [noble]∧⌜fortunate⌝ a son, & merited by it.

Enter A Constable & officers

Con: Thatꝭ the man ap^{r}phend him. | *They lay hands on wild* |

Enter Thrifty & Parchm^{t}.

Thrif: Thatꝭ he, the principall accessary, & the accessarie
Principall

Pet: yor wor^{ps} ithe right S^{r}, he did abet, as yo^{u} haue
oath for it.

[*Th*] *mũ.* If *Iustice Thrifty* had not bene in ꝑson, I must needs
haue said, yo^{u} had wrongd me and this gentleman
in the course of salutacon.

wild If one may speake at a time, & not anoth^{r} interrupt
him wch is not all wayes ꝑmitted among Iustices of
peace, I [onely] as a man specially interested desire
⌜to know⌝ a reason of my app^{r}hension.

Thrif: O simple fellow, a delinquent examine a Iustice of peace
gooder & gooder as I told yo^{u} before, he that asks me

[FOL. 126 p. 22]

22

a reason Ile committ him for that & so take him away wth
out bayle or maine prise. 126

wild. If I had met wth executioners that [had] had bene but
as well bred as a french dog wth 2 noses, or a maiestrat
[that had had but as]⌜of abilitie⌝ wthout haueing his clerk [as] [a] ⌜to be his⌝
prompter, I should haue born my restraint wth lesse
[im] sense of abuse. | *Exeunt Officers & wild* |

Thrif: An incorrigible [fellow] ⌜impudence⌝ as I told you before

Sop: For my sake S^{r} haue pity on that gentleman,
perhaps when yo^{u} were yong a suppliant
Of [my] meaner ꝑtꝭ might haue p^{r}uayled wth yo^{u}.

Thrif: I grant it Lady but ⌜now⌝ my [yeares are [stirrd] inclin'd] ⌜needle stirrs⌝
⌜The trembling point⌝ ⌜coole North pole⌝

1817 *[noble]∧*] caret positioned under *bl* 1837 *[had]*] heavily scored out 1846–53 *I grant ... selfe*] original version reads: *I grant it Lady but my yeares are stirrd* [revised to *inclin'd*] | *Rather to grant* [revised to *heare*] *requestꝭ of grauitie* | *Then suitꝭ of youth & beauty. had yor moth^{r}* | *Commanded Iustice Thrifty, he would fortwth* | *Haue cryd yor seruant worthy m^{ris} mumble* | *But for yor selfe.* This was revised to: *I grant it Lady but now my needle stirrs* | *The trembling point to this wholsom coole North pole* | *And feares a yonger torrid Zone like wildfire*; *Then ... moth^{r}* not cancelled when passage revised, but probably should be 1846 *needle stirrs*] interlined above *yeares are [stirrd]*

[Rather to [grant] [⌜heare⌝] requestꝭ of grauitie] to this wholsom
Then suitꝭ of youth & beauty. had yor moth^{r}
[Commanded Iustice Thrifty, he would fortwth]
⌜And feares a yonger torrid Zone like wildfire⌝
[Haue cryd yor seruant worthy m^{ris} mumble]
[But for yor selfe]

Sop: pray ⌜what⌝ for me good S^{r}.

Thrif: I wish yo^{u} had yor mothers wealth & me yor lawfull∧ ⌜or legitimate⌝
husband, & there were no offence to *Justice*.

mum. What sayes he, what sayes he?
⌜stands ticklish vpon the sere clap but down⌝

Thrif: I say youth [is a dangerous thing to meddle wth, &]
[wh] [staydnes is a good thing in all kind of conuersa=]
[tion.] a button snap it goes of like a stone bow or a gun

mũ. Truly it dos so. | new oyld

Sop: Pray mother strayne yor selfe to speake a word
for the gentleman, I wonder yor hart bleeds not to
see him so vsd.

Thrif: yo^{u} shall cōmand me so I may haue the next wish
after, truly good m^{ris} mumble.

mum: I haue cause m^{r} Thrifty [for that] if yo^{u} knew all.
indeed he comes to be a suiter to my daughter, vpon
ones cōmendacōn that loues yo^{u} & yo^{r}ꝭ, though yo^{u} be
somwhat awcord to him, but let that rest,

Thrif: Well but as yo^{u} told me

mum. I, as I was saying, this m^{r} Wild I suspected to be
a suiter to me, but consider⌜ing⌝ that green∧ ⌜woood⌝ was nought
to put into a [crached] ⌜crazed⌝ house, & [vpo] ag^{t} any ill wea=
ther [would]∧ ⌜will⌝ crack & shrink from the old building
I sufferd him, I mary did I, to ask *Sophia* a question,
& me thought the couple were in a p^{r}ty forwardnes
for the time, yong folks togeth^{r} m^{r} Thrifty, euen so it
should be.

Thrif: And do yo^{u} think there were any hurt for old folks
to be togeth^{r} too?

1862 *dos*] *o* over *i*; original reading *is* *new oyld*] positioned as in MS; perhaps a late addition as written in same slightly lighter ink as insertion at 1847 1874 ⌜*woood*⌝] spelled as in MS 1876 *[would]*∧] caret positioned under *u*

mũ: Less danger by much,
Thrif: Then let yor old neighbo^{r}, & yor true freind, & as I told
yo^{u} before a man in authority, euen my selfe in ꝓ ꝑ
ꝑson be bold to make the motion.
mũ. O good m^{r} Thrifty. pray speake loud this bussling
has made my head sing y^{t} [my]‸⌜me⌝ thinks my heareing
fayles me
So: S^{r} wthout a more continued cruelltye
[Disn] Release the worthy gentleman, my word
Shall be his bayle, if yo^{u} will please to take it
Thrif: Will yo^{u} be bound body for body.
So. Had I desert to be an equall prize
[To gaine his safety.]
For his deare safety, or might ransome him
Wth tender or aduenture of [h] my life
And all those poore thingꝭ y^{t} haue [a relation] ⌜any reference⌝
To my safe being, nature was not more liberall
In lending me my breath, then I should be
[L] Forward in retribution of y^{t} debt
⌜pay't this instant⌝
His bounty [bound] ⌜made⌝ me [to] ⌜owe⌝ to [pay't[it]‸ quickly]
To gaine assurance of his p^{r}seruation.
mũ. please yo^{u} to drink m^{r} Thrifty.
Thrif: Good m^{ris} mumble I thank yo^{u}
mũ. Will yo^{u} not so, pray drink S^{r}.
Thrif: yes if yo^{u} please.
mũ. Godfry, hearke hither Godfry. [*She talks wth Godfrye.*]
Thrif: The truth is m^{ris} *Sophia* I haue
a mind of yor moth^{r} m^{r} Wild of yo^{u}
mũ. yo^{u} heare me Godfrye
Thrif: It seemes, & yo^{u} are so courteous as not to
requite him wth disdayne, ⌜&⌝ as I told yo^{u} before
worke yo^{u} wth yor moth^{r} for me
mũ. I the siluer [tankard]‸⌜spout pot⌝ *Godfry*.

1887 *bussling*] pronounced gap between *buss* and *ling* 1888 *[my]‸*] caret positioned under *my* *thinks*] *t* over *c*? reading uncertain 1890–1926 *S^{r} ... certaine*] intermittent vertical line runs between speech prefixes and dialogue in same ink as is used on rest of page 1897 *[h]*] only partly formed 1903 *pay't[it]‸*] *'t* squeezed in; caret positioned under *ay* 1916 *[tankard]‸*] caret positioned under *ka*

Thrif: And m^{r} Wild shall be at yor dispose.
mum. Now go yor wayes *Godfry*. [*Exit*]
Sop. S^{r} there are some other accidentꝭ falln out
wch my moth^{r} will acquaint yo^{u} wth her selfe
Some thingꝭ past help vnles yo^{u} be discreet
If so in happy forwardnes to be
Gone on wth comfort [to]
mum. Come againe *Godfry* bring the damask drinking
napkin, if [owers]∧⸢wooers⸣ be not well vsd theyl come the
seldomer of a certaine
Godf: yes forsooth *Exit Godfrye*
Sop: my mother will declare how all thingꝭ stand S^{r}.
Thrif: And m^{ris} mumble as I told yo^{u} before, the case being
[stands] thus&I [being]∧⸢my selfe⸣ Iustice of peace in three

[Fol. 127 p. 23]

127 23 [33]

counties besides middlesex, & [Iu] of oyer & terminer
all the Western circuit besides am willing [wth yor]
[leaue sufferance licence & ꝑmission] to make yo^{u} [the] ⸢wife⸣
to the right wor^{p}full & then yo^{u} may goe before any
lawyers wife i the parish.
mũ. Good m^{r} Thrifty I thank yor kindnes S^{r}, but an vnfor=
tunate boy of mine I heare has offended yo^{u} S^{r}; & I
must take motherly pity, & respect mine own flesh &
blood∧⸢in my match⸣ Kit Spruse yo^{u} know is so S^{r}.
Thrif: As I told yo^{u} before m^{ris} mumble, thingꝭ must be as
they may when they can be no oth^{r}wise, & for safety
sake a iudiciall rep^{r}hension shall serue ⸢the yong cople⸣ but no par=
ting now I assure yo^{u}, & though authority be hot
when it is incenst, yet Iustice is∧⸢euer⸣ coole at the lat=
ter end of a [busines] ⸢day⸣, & yor son Kester & my daughter
Constance let hem een breed now they ha ioynd, Ile
make her portion as good as his, [&c. &c.] ⸢since now shes not⸣
mũ. Vpon yor word S^{r}. fit for any other man
Thrif: Vpon my worpfull word as I told yo^{u} before.
Enter Godfry wth wine & bisket bread.

1925 *[owers]*∧] caret positioned under *ow* 1930 *thus&I*] spacing suggests & a late addition 1945 ⸢*euer*⸣] over previously interlined and smudged *vsually* 1948–9 ⸢*since . . . man*] *since . . . not* interlined above cancelled *&c. &c.*; *fit . . . man* fitted after Mumble's reply

mũ. Nay Godfry now weel take more time to drink
o^{r} sack, [in], carry it in again good Godfry, my old frend
proues my good freind.

Sop: One word [as I to] for m^{r} [Spruce] ⌜Wild⌝ I beseech yo^{u} S^{r} heare
me.

Thrif: Peter as I told yo^{u} before let m^{r} [Spruse]^ ⌜Wild⌝ be set at
large.

Pet. He shall be manumitted wthout fees, if one word
do not signify, the oth^{r} sounds contentedly to any
gallant in England. *Exit*

mũ. Nay now yo^{u} shew yor selfe, as yo^{u} are m^{r} Thrifty.

Thrif. A man of power in my diuision as I told yo^{u} before.
& a [fellow]^ ⌜gentleman⌝ well bred at the vniu^{r}sality of meetingꝭ *Exeunt.*

Enter will. Catch. Tom Snap.

Catch. Barr hanging & the Emperors [li] territoris are but
a yonger broth^{r}ꝭ portion to o^{r}ꝭ, & the great *Mogull*
is [youth] not yet out of his wardship, [we are born]
[free & come] ⌜*computatis computandis.*⌝

Snap. Pish, we are born free & come to o^{r} estates wthout
sueing a liuery.
⌜Thatꝭ the reason that if we giue any of the officers a pint⌝

Catch. [I think] thou & [I may curse the Clerk, & to be reuen=]
[ged heel^ [⌜make k^{t}ꝭ stand bare in his office &⌝] sweare at honester men.]
⌜of wine, theyl accept it of grace, not exact it of due.⌝

[Snap:] [Fy particulars keep mood & figure els yor sillogisme]

Snap. ⌜True & yo^{u} may call any of hem knaues, & their guilt [& yor]⌝
[will be ridiculous]; [but stand close I heare company]
⌜& yor independence, will free yo^{u} from being told you mistake⌝
[*They bend their pistolls.*]
⌜the man but stand close I here companye.⌝
⌜*They bend their pistolls.*⌝

1957 *[Spruse]^*] caret positioned under *ru* 1964 *[fellow]^*] caret positioned under *lo* 1966 *[li]*] smudged out; reading uncertain 1968 *[we ... born]*] heavily smudged; reading uncertain 1969 *[free & come]*] heavily smudged; reading uncertain 1972–5 *Thatꝭ ... due*] speech originally read *I think thou & I may curse the Clerk, & to be reuen= | ged heel sweare at honester men.*; this was expanded by interlining *make k^{t}ꝭ stand bare in his office &* with a caret after *heel*. These lines were then cancelled, and 1972 and 1975 interlined to read *Thatꝭ the reason that if we giue any of the officers a pint | of wine, theyl accept it of grace, not exact it of due.* The uncancelled *thou &* at 1973 is probably an oversight. 1976–82 *[Fy ... pistolls.⌝]* original reading was *Fy particulars keep mood & figure els yor sillogisme | will be ridiculous; but stand close I heare company | They bend their pistolls.* This was cancelled, and the following speech interlined: *True & yo^{u} may call any of hem knaues, & their guilt & yor* [*& yor* cancelled] | *& yor independence, will free yo^{u} from being told you mistake | the man but stand close I here companye. | They bend their pistolls.* The revised stage direction is squeezed into the space at the bottom of the page.

[Fol. 127v p. 23v]

Enter Spruse, Constance, & [⟨ ⟩] Crisp wth
a chest of bottles.

Spr. Now that o^{r} minds haue varied their intentions
Care made them to much sub^{t} to, & solitude
X Euills ꝑswader, groweing in dislike
[Of] ⌜Wth⌝ [o^{r}] the reciprocall [happines] [o^{r} m] ⌜acceptation⌝
And mutuall [retribution] ⌜[giuen] rendring of religious dues⌝ [wch we offer]
[Of the religious rites wch chastitie] ⌜W^{ch} loue receaues & giues⌝
[And loue receaue & take]. Let imitation
Of men recorded for their graue dispose
That stroue to giue a needfull moderation
And did compell the too intentiue minds
Of labouring mortalitie to recreate
Their wearied faculties, make vs [true obseruers] ⌜strict solemnizers⌝
Of those designed holy dayes their wisdome
⌜the same dayes institution⌝
Thought fit [to] ⌜should⌝ haue [an m] [concomitant creation]
wth lawes of kingdomes in the instant point
Of time & [order] order; Had they bene [ex] eye witnesses
They must haue wth ingenious recognition
[Haue granted] ⌜Acknowledged⌝, we haue had a great^{r} share
Of sad disquiet, then their [pitifull intentions] ⌜mercy did [p] [intend]⌝
Intend should giue man a capacitie
To reape this beneficiall ease.
[*Sop*] *Con:* Deare S^{r}.
For all those heauy sufferingꝭ wch I
Haue bene expos'd‸ ⌜to⌝, this [s] [glad] howre makes amends,
Spr. Nay then my dearely honourd, when we [are] ⌜shall⌝ be
Blest wth a quick arriue, at that faire pallace
wch an howers trauaill more will lead vs to
And consum̃ation of o^{r} nuptiall ioyes
Shall by the goodnes of solemnitie
Giue vs‸ ⌜the⟨t⟩ [the]⌝ freedome to express o^{r} thoughtꝭ

1983 *[⟨ ⟩]*] reading uncertain; looks like a looped ascender, but letter not fully formed 1986 *made*] *m* over what looks like ascender 1988–91 *[Of] . . . take*] original reading: *Of o^{r}* [revised to *the*] *reciprocall happines* | *And mutuall retribution wch we offer* | *Of the religious rites wch chastitie* | *And loue receaue & take*. This was revised to: *Wth the reciprocall acceptation* | *And mutuall rendring of religious dues* | *W^{ch} loue receaues & giues*. 1989 ⌜*[giuen] . . . dues*⌝] positioned over *retribution . . . offer* 1993 *giue*] *i* over *a* 2015 *the⟨t⟩ [the]*] terminal *t* of *thet* seems probable, but obscured by ink blot

In liberall[,] [ch] action, changing starud conceipt
[To] Into the highfed execution
Of things [in explic] wch weake exp^{r}ssion hath not power
To make vs vnderstand. yor own beleefe
Will like yor selfe make [yor] ⌜a⌝ confession
Free & ingenious
Catch. [*Ca*] I am not taken wth this oratory.
Snap: Stay let vs [take] ⌜catch⌝ 'hem at the best aduantage.
There's no time lost.
Sp: The coṁendable vse w^{ch} [noblemen] ⌜greatest Princes⌝
Ease themselues in their iournyes wth I haue
(Tender of yor safe being) bene p^{r}sumpt[ions]⌜uous⌝
To put in practise. *Crisp* the chest of bottles
Cris: Here S^{r}.
Sp. As for yor ease & recreation
yo^{u} pleasd to leaue the coach, & make ye surface
Of this blest place, to thank yo^{u} for depressing

[Fol. 128 p. 24]

24

Those [thankfull] ⌜humble⌝ [herbs] blades of grass, wch rise againe
As gratefull sub^{t}(when their soueraignes hand 128
Takes of the yoake of seruitude. so now
A vouchafe at my intreatie to receaue
A spoonefull of restoring wine, pure spirit
Of pearle & amber are the sole ingredient(
The liquor viper wine, rarely infusd by artificiall skill
Con: I that durst trust yo^{u}
Thus farr will not refuse a courtesie
[w^{c}] That yo^{u} coṁend.
Sp: Dick *Crisp*, powre out some wine
But wth such carefull diligence the spirit(
Loose not their strength.

Catch & Snap. discouer themselues.

Catch. Sirrha first deliuer yo^{u} what yo^{u} haue. [*to Crisp:*]
about yo^{u}.
Snap: Gentleman & Lady, the old saying need breakes
stone walls, teacheth yo^{u} what to doe. [*To them*]

2022 [*Ca*]] positioned as in MS   2051 *To them*] right-hand descender of box is a curled brace

Cris: Truly S^{r} I haue nothing but this chest of strong
waters & my box of instrum^{t}ꝭ wch I surrender |*Exit*
Sp: I am sorry that two thingꝭ so noblye borne
As will & resolution should be [misvs'd] ⌜so much abus'd⌝
Catch. A man can hardly grow fat wth eating stones,
nor will a taylor be payd, wth crying excuse me
S^{r}, time has bene we ha thought it scuruy to
goe wth o^{r} hayres vnpowdred, & [thought]‸⌜bene of opinion⌝ a twelfe
peny ordnary or a cookes shop would make a man
⌜or lowsy if his cloke did sweep of the stall⌝
stink wth lookeing into, but now S^{r}, euery man
for himselfe, for his being, that he may eat, &
not cry tis for my reputation, those were
thingꝭ once but now, S^{r} I assure yo^{u} the belly
thatꝭ hungry will not find fault wth his taylor
for makeing his clothes out of fashion, [&] a man
must be before he can be a gallant, one is es=
sentiall, the oth^{r} is but a kin to circũstance
I [can assure] ⌜am plaine wth⌝ yo^{u} yo^{u} must change doubletꝭ wth me.
Snap. And breeches wth me.
Sp: Shall I secure this Lady then.
Catch. All but her clothes & Iewells.
Con Take all good gentlemen onely spare my life.
Snap: O that it were as it has bene that I might vsher
yo^{u} to a play or be yor seruant to the stillyard Lady
but the more cross are the starrs tis not so happy.
but as yo^{u} sayd Lady yor iewells.
Sp: Her iewells how yo^{u} [curr] ⌜slaue⌝, fly for yor safety, these two
barking currs, I'l quiet wth as much [ease] ⌜facility⌝ as if I were
at any sport I [take delight in]. loue

[FOL. 128v p. 24v]

Spruse offers to fight wth them
Catch. Are yo^{u} so gamsome what fence haue yo^{u} for
this. |*Shewes a pistoll.*
Snap. Or this.
Spr Nay then I doe beseech yo^{u} fly as fast
As yor ability can help yo^{u} forward,
[*Spr.*] Those starrs that are inclind to mercy keepe
yor passage safe.

2054 *noblye*] *ye* over *e*

Catch. Lady we are content, humanity
Dwells in o^{r} brestꝭ, though hard [pinching] ⌜necessity⌝ need,
Constrayne[s] vs to vse violence, one iewell
shall make yor ransome. *She giues a iewell*
Con. As yo^{u} haue bene cõpassionate [on] ⌜to⌝ me
Shew equall mercy to this gentleman.
Snap: We are not safe o^{r}selues this wayles place
Doth lye obnoxious to diuersitye
Of dangers & is liable to more
Then vs of this condicõn; if yo^{u} desire
To [safe] ⌜saue⌝ yor life away.
Con: Tis a hard choise
To [h] die in p^{r}sent or to [hope] ⌜looke⌝ for death
wth in an howers space, ꝑhaps a minutes
Farewell the best the noblest gentleman
That euer had misfortune by a woman,
If thou escapst consult wth euery path
W^{ch} way I went Ile write my sad cõplaintꝭ
Vpon some silent solitarie tree
And set 'hem to the tune of *Lacrymæ.* *Exit*
Sp: I am insensible els I had ꝑceaud
The power y^{t} left me, yo^{u} may exercise
All the tormenting [cruellties] ⌜violence⌝ yo^{u} please
Or cruelltie can think of, my disast^{r}ꝭ
[Are] ⌜Haue⌝ past the height of their extremitie
And duld my app^{r}hension that I cannot
perceaue iniurious vsage.
Catch. Of wth yor doublet, So. *He puts of his doublet*
Snap: yor breeches too S^{r}.
Spr: I beseech yo^{u} gentlemen.
Catch. Empty yor buttond pocket then & we
Will fauour yo^{u} so much as to dismiss yo^{u}.
Spr: As I [am] ⌜loue⌝ vertue there is all I haue
And if yo^{u} will but retribute one peece
To beare [but]∧ ⌜a⌝ [one]∧ ⌜sad⌝ nightꝭ charges if kind fate
[Doe] ⌜shall⌝ make y^{t} honourd gentle⌜womã⌝(yo^{u} saw

2091 ⌜*necessity*⌝ *need*] redundancy in MS *if*] over smudged word that is possibly *if* 2115 *duld*] terminal *d* over *l* 2124 *[but]*∧] caret positioned under *u* 2125 *gentle*⌜*womã*⌝*(yo^{u}*] *man* adjusted to read *womã* (*m* changed to *w*; *a* to *o*; *n* to *m*; *ã* fitted in space between *man* and *(yo^{u}*

part in such discontent) & me to meet
Againe, Ile owe yo^{u} double thankꝭ.
Catch. What a braue thing it is to be the bett^{r} man
Broth^{r} what sayst?
Snap. Thou knowst what want will driue a good man
too, & theres no such vexation‸ ⌜as⌝ to meet wth a

[FOL. 129 p. 25]

25

mans wench, & want mony to pay for her supꝑ.
Spr. As I liue, that religious innocent 129
Is my betrothed wife.
Snap: Here take a peece againe
Catch. Giue him a *Iack* [or a *Carolus*], for thou knowest
none but lawrells will goe [amongst‸ o^{r} fraternity.] ⌜in o^{r} companye.⌝
Snap: Tis done fare ye well S^{r}.
Spr: Farewell kind gentleman.
Spruse walks one way they another.
Catch: Come share, share, *Enter the 3 other theeues*
Care: Halfe o^{r}ꝭ, or stand *Careles, Kilman, Dingthrift.*
Snap: Theeues among o^{r} selues, nay then tis time to leaue
the trade.
Ding: yeeld or try whose pistolls will hit best
Catch. you'r three to two.
Kil: We vnderstand it S^{r}, & wth out expostulation expect
Halfe, or els weele charge.
Care: yeeld or draw, tis faire.
Guard ye we are impatient, yo^{u} do not meet wth
a gentleman vsher & his Lady here. *They fighting*
They let fall Spruses doublet. *Exeunt.*
Sp: Nay then ꝑhaps this is a good portent
Of future safety. *Puts it on againe.*
when a man is sad
Tis sin to cherish melancholy, raise
Thy low brought spiritꝭ, seeke thy louely m^{ris}
wth eyes of inquisition, & a mind
prompted wth zealous earnestnes. but O
my spiritꝭ fayle me, when I doe repeat

2138 *amongst‸*] caret positioned under *gs* 2160 *earnestnes.*] two faint comma-like marks under *n* and terminal *s*

Her name & am debarrd the looking on
So braue an obiect I must please my selfe
And [sacrifise]^ ⌜sacrifice⌝ to her before I moue. *Enter Crisp.*
Cris: How doe yo^{u} S^{r}?
[P] Spr: O thou stinking coward
Leaue me in an extremitie.
Cris: My loss is most S^{r}, for all my liuingꝭ gone
my boxe of siluer instrum^{t}ꝭ.
Spr. All the^ ⌜black⌝ curses that [were ere] ⌜haue bene⌝ produc'd
by [obsecration] ⌜inuocation⌝ light on thee & them.
wher[e] are the theeues.
Cris: Gone S^{r} I had not stirrd els.
Spr: Art thou sure?
Cris: Am I sure Im here S^{r}, I assure yor wo^{rp}, I peepd
as long as I could see a man, before I crept
out of the hollow tree.
Spr: Plague o yor creeping, & wheres the Lady *Constance*
Cris: Truly yo^{u} pose me now S^{r}, all my drift, was but
to saue yor wo^{rps} barbers skin, who should ha trim̃d
you if I had been killd.

[Fol. 129v p. 25v]

Sp: O thou dull slaue respect mortalitie
And let an Angell slip thy obseruation
Humanity mistakes, [we] ⌜I⌝ greeue not as
[I am] [obligd]^ [⌜bound,⌝] ⌜I [will] [must]⌝ [accom̃odate thy [⌜my⌝] sorrow]
⌜I am bound I must accommodate my sorrow⌝
Not as the customary weeꝑs mourn
That whine for fashion, but as the noble thing
[Thou art]^ ⌜I am⌝ depriu'd of calls for. *Crisp come* hither.
Go looke the woods, & euery formall tree
That giues thee salutation take by th' hand
And ask it how it does?
Cris: Why I beseech yo^{u} S^{r}?
Spr: If the tree make a leg^ ⌜wilt not⌝ thou [mayst] put of thy hat?
Cris: That I shall S^{r}.

2164 *[sacrifise]^*] caret positioned under *c* 2185 *I am ... sorrow*] original reading: *I am obligd* [revised to *bound*] *accom̃odate thy* [revised to *my*] *sorrow*; *I will* [revised to *must*] interlined with caret before *accom̃odate*; line with its interlineations then cancelled and newly revised version interlined below ⌜*I [will] [must]*⌝] *I* probably overlooked for deletion
2189 *art]^*] caret positioned under *ar*

Spr. Except yor m^{r} be at the same time likely to be
robbd & then you'l run away.
Cris: O I beseech yo^{u} S^{r} I rememb^{r} it to my greefe.
Spr. And yo^{u} haue seene a tree make a leg I know.
Cris: Vpon yor wo^{rps} word I take it S^{r}.
Spr: Very good S^{r} yo^{u} are a freind at need; youl tell
a lye to make yor m^{r} merry, or sweare a thing
because his wor^{p} sayes it, yo^{u} that would leaue
me [when yor] then, Ile turn‸⌜[you]⌝ away now.
Cris No I beseech yo^{u} S^{r}.|S. yes truly. *Cris.* Deare S^{r}‸⌜yor⌝ pardon
& try my seruice once more
Spr: Then heare yor charge and wth as quick a vigilance[⟨ ⟩]
As [yo] ⌜thou⌝ wouldststriue to get thy pardon signed
Wert thou to die to morow, range the woods
Leaue not a sheepheards boy vnquestiond
That can but tell his sheep, let not a milkmaid
Escape thine inquisition, & all other meanes
Be earnest in whereby I may be satisfyed
[The] [wth but one single particle of tidings]
[Conc] Of Constance or her fortunes.
Cris: I goe S^{r}
Theeues miss me & Im happy. |*Exit*.
Spr: How many thousand hipocrites do shed
Their teares, that the compassionate spectato^{r}ℓ
[Al] may say Im sory for hem, And as many
Do drie their eyes when [not a] ⌜theres no⌝ looker on
[Is]‸⌜To be a⌝ witnes of their [lamentation]. suffering
[Thinking] ⌜Esteeming⌝ it [as] a gross absurditie
Not to weepe when anoth^{r}ℓ sad occasion
Inuites them to't for cõpany. but I
Need not a cue to prompt me, my calamitie
Hangℓ not vpon the approbation [of] of
[Of] Anoth^{r} mans opinion, here it lyes
That scorns, a fiction; when a reall torm^{t}
Contendswthin the heart must burst or yeeld
[Or]‸⌜Ile⌝ seeke a healeing remedie tis she

2205–6 *S. yes ... more*] addition fitted into space provided by Crisp's half-line speech 2205 *S^{r}*‸] caret positioned under *r* 2207 *vigilance[⟨ ⟩]* terminal letter blotted out 2208 *wouldststriue*] first *st* squeezed between *would* and *striue* 2230 *Contendswthin*] *s* squeezed between *Contend* and *wthin* 2231 *[Or]*‸] caret positioned under *r*

That wth the *Elixir* of hir pure [desertꝭ] apparance
must make me liue, thou feminine maiestie
Looke on me wth thy splendor, that I may

[FOL. 130 p. 26]

26

Haue one occasion more to thank kind nature
For lending me mine eyes. | *Exit* 130

Enter some sheepheards.

King: For my yeare & in o^{r} sheepwalks, [there is not a] ⌜*Pan* was neuer⌝ more
absolute king, nor‸ ⌜is⌝ there a better gouernd cõmon
wealth in [Christendome then o^{r}ꝭ] ⌜Christendome then o^{r}s⌝. [*Arcadia* it selfe.]

1 Sh: Nay thatꝭ wthout all ꝑaduenture.

King. you are all of that mind.

All. All, all.

2 Sh: I am of that mind too, but I dare not say so for
feare of displeaseing my Landlord for he sayes
his wor^{p} being a Iustice of peace keepes the beg=
gers in bett^{r} order, & the alehouses in a more for=
mall subiection, then the king of sheepheards his
vnder dealers.

King. Who thy Landlord?

2 Sh: yes his good wor^{p} king

King. I will rebuke him p^{r}sently, & shew thee what a
poore ordinary thing a Iustice is now, that stu=
dies statute [more, then downright honestie]
yet must not doe as the law leads for feare of
displeaseing, my Lord his next neighbour that
tooke in the Cōmon.

3 Sh. O I know who that is.

King. I but when yor king speakes, yo^{u} must neuer cry
any thing but good, or well spoken, or admirable
or so, neuer disturb him, but cry king goe on, or
bless o^{r} gou^{r}no^{r}.

1 Sh: The king sayes true of a certaine.

King: Then sub^{t}ꝭ be content, when yo^{u} are required wthout
runing away,‸ ⌜to⌝ put yor cambrells quietly into the

2232–4 *That ... may*] two indistinct pencil marks in margin, both hatched over in ink
2266 *cambrells*] *r* over cancelled letter with looped ascender

hooke of [gou^{r}m^{t}]∧⌜restraint⌝, struggle not when yor kingꝭ dog catches yo^{u} by th' eare, though he pinch it quite through [till] ⌜or make⌝ the blood come, be not vnwilling to receaue the pitchbrand of [distinguishm^{t},] ⌜distinction,⌝ though ye iron be so hot it make yor buttock⟨ ⟩ blister, are yo^{u} content?

All. yes very well content

King. Then draw cuttꝭ who shall pipe to day, the rest shall dig a sheepheards table to set on o^{r} flawnes & sillibubs

1. Sh. Will goodmans turn & dick [sheepheards] ⌜*Hoppers*⌝ *They draw*

King: Set then set. *Enter A musician*

Mus: Is the king of sheepheards pleasd to heare good mu= sick, & a song y^{ts} newly set, an excellent∧ ⌜new⌝ song ant please yo^{u}.

King Stay a little fellow take yor spades & about yor work

they make a sheepheards table.

[Fol. 130v p. 26v]

King: How dare yo^{u} trauell that are rogues by th' statute & Iustices dwell at euery town y^{t} [want fellowes] ⌜dare meddle wth⌝ [to shew their authority vpon].∧/ ⌜nothing but whipping of beggers.⌝

1.Sh. I beseech thee good king let them play, & then may we dance euery one wth his wench, we can pipe at any time minstrells come not euery day.

King. They shall they shall. Draw fellows draw.

mus: A very good new song too an youl heare it.

King. Songꝭ we in the country take songꝭ to be parills thingꝭ they say such as yo^{u} ha bene whipt for songꝭ.

mus: Fooles they fooles they, y^{t} knew not what they said.

King. Can yo^{u} sing a song among vs if a good brest teach yo^{u} o^{r} tune, some on vs can write, & the words are of o^{r} own makeing pure mountaine *Poetry*.

Mus: Yes p^{r}sently.

⌜*as many*⌝ ⌜*[5] [or] [6]*⌝ ⌜*as shepheards*⌝
Enter [2 or 3] country wenches∧ wth prouision.

2267 *[gou^{r}m^{t}]∧*] caret positioned under *o* 2271 *buttock⟨ ⟩*] terminal letter blotted and illegible 2285 ∧/] thin line extending down from interlineation reinforces placement of revision 2298–9 ⌜*as many … prouision*] order of revision: *5 or 6* interlined above cancelled *2 or 3*, then cancelled; *as many* inserted to left of *5 or 6*. Thin line extending from *as many* to left of cancelled *2 or 3* below reinforces intended placement. Final reading: *Enter as many country wenches as shepheards wth prouision* 2298 ⌜*as shepheards*⌝] positioned above *wenches*

King: Here Sirrha let yor boy get that by heart to this
tune ⌊*He sings.*
And do yo^{u} play, while we eat Come sit down all
fellowes all fellowes, onely by my place I am
this day to haue a wench to my selfe, & I choose
Tib. ⌊*Kisseth her.*
Euery man els his wench in his turn,

1 Sh. I madge white.
2 Shep. I bes blackabye. [*They all sit downe & eat. Musick playes.*]
3 Shep. Kit Harrison come.
4 Shep By yor leaue Iylion.
5 Shep. Bony Kate thy hand
King. Strike vp Lads. wellcome all.
1 Shep. O what meat is cheese cake, & yet gentlemen
are so mad as feed chickens wth corne
2 Shep [And] I an we were as mad as they, how should
we do for mony to∧⌜buy⌝ [by] new stock after a rot yeare.
King. Where had yo^{u} this ale Tib.
[*Ti*]*Tib.* At mother brewers King, she's a clanly woman,
drink much good de yor good heart.
King. I ha had a sound pluck at it.
Tib. Shall we ha nere a daunce King.
King. yy but we haue a song to sing, first Lad art rea=
dy.
Boy. yes now when yo^{u} please
King. And to o^{r} own tune.
Boy. yor own tune to a haire yo^{u} shall heare [*Boy sings.*
[*Boy*] Very excellent begin stripling weele euery one
King. haue a ꝑt [*He begins*
Too high I cannot reach. [*Boy takes it lower.*
So. But sirrha least yo^{u} should not sing right come yo^{u} in
wth ye Chorus, & play the tune o yor fiddles, & Ile sing y^{e}

[FOL. 131 p. 27]

27

song my selfe. *They play he sings.* 131

While∧⌜harmles⌝ sheepheards watch their flocks
In mirth & iollitye

2316 *new*] apostrophe-like form positioned over *n* shown here

2333 *131*] archivist's page number fitted in half-line lower than

The sounding ecchoes of the rocks
Increase their melodye

No troubleous or tormenting care
Can obscure the geniall day
Appointed to receaue the faire
Inuiters of their play
Tib.
1 Shep: *Madge*
2 Shep: *Bes*
3 Sh: *Kit*
4 Sh: *Iil*
5 Sh. *and Kate*
All *These are the lasses we*
Must not refuse to get at any rate
To increase o^{r} harmonye.
Chorꝰ: *Tib. &c*
Kin: *We need no Ladies of the court*
That laugh their Lords to scorne
Who to afford their seruants sport
Make their husbands weare the horne

O^{r} homely wenches of the downes
Are more delightsome farr
And weare their comely pleated gownes
More hansome & these are
Tib.
1 Sh: *Madge. &c:*
All. *The iouiall lasses we*
Must not refuse to get at any rate
To increase o^{r} harmonye.
Kin. *We need no city tradesmens wiues*
They looke too much in glasses
And [Who] lead themselues such Ladies wiues
They make their husbands asses.

[FOL. 131v p. 27v]

Our sweet breath'd wenches looking glass
Is a cleare open spring

2367 *wiues*] *w* over ascending stroke; original letter indiscernible

Where euery one suruayes her face
While her sweet heart doth merryly sing
Tib.
1 Sh. *Madge.*
2 Sh. *Bes*
3 Sh. *Kit*
4 Sh. *Iil*
5 Sh. *and Kate*
All *These are the lasses we*
Must not refuse to get at any rate
To increase o^{r} *[melo] harmonye.*
Chor^{9}*:* *Tib. &c.*
King play lads *Enter Cruch his wife & M*^{ris} *Constance.* *Musick playes*
Cruch. Certaynly I know not the way
[*old wom:*]⌜*Con:*⌝Nor yo^{u} old mother?
old. wo. I neuer was a mile from home this 52 yeare
but like a thirty yeare agoe I went to London
to see my daughter grace that maryed a water
man, it was like a 30 yeare a goe, Thomas.
⌜tis not a moone vnder or ore it was about⌝
Cruch. yy much about margery [but whence come]
[ye gentlewoman] ⌜11 yeare afore captaine pouch, & we had bene⌝
then maried an 28 yeare, ye red cow wth one
horn died while we ⌜were⌝ from whome, but whence
come ye gentlewoman.
Con: It would abide a long discourse to tell yo^{u}
All the sad chances I haue vndergone,
And by what vnexpected miracle
I light vpon yo^{u}.
Cruch. How sa.
old wõ: And whither woud ye.
Con: To any [place]‸⌜village⌝ that is but hospitable
⌜in my desires⌝⌜[I] [ayme at [is]⌝⌜most]⌝

2381 *[melo]*] reading uncertain; *o* only partly formed and might be *s* 2386 *[old wom:]*] *old* smudged; *wom:* crossed out 2393⌜*11 ... bene*⌝] interlined above *ye gentlewoman*, but insertion joins main line after *captaine* 2404–7⌜*in ... house*] passage originally read *yet the selected place my own desires | most appetitiously do ayme at is | One m*^{r} *Wellcomes house.* Then *my ... is* cancelled and *I ayme at is* [revised to *most*] interlined with caret; *ayme at most* cancelled; *most earnestly desire*

yet the selected place^ [my own desires]
[most appetitiously do ayme at is] ⌜[most earnestly desire to come to is]⌝
[One]^ ⌜Is⌝ m^{r} Wellcomes house.
Old wom. yo^{u} were lap'd in yor mothers smock
That is his shepheard.
King. father Cruch wellcome will yo^{u} takepart?
Cruch. Thank ye heartyly your king this yeare

[Fol. 132 p. 28]

King: For fault of a ƀre fath^{r} Cruch, yo^{u} know places 28.
of trust & com̃and are not allwayes put into the 132
hands of men of desert, as for example the Consta=
ble of o^{r} [par] ⌜town⌝ this yeare is a foole, the next Iust=
tice of peace is a I mary is he, the Sheriffe of
the countye a man of good clothes, & the Lord[s]
of^ ⌜the⌝ manner com̃only an elder brother, [& I king of the]
[Shepheards.]
⌜The K. of shepheard sure hath bene a herald⌝
Con: [Sure]^ [yo^{u} haue] [bene some] [herald][s] [man]
[yo^{u}]^ ⌜He⌝ dos dispose men & their true descriptions
In such a proꝑ series.
King. I haue my walks from that hill to y^{t} Dingle, from
y^{t} bush to the other thick thorns, if a sheep leap
out of order my dog giues him a fecth a gaine
or my whistle a recall, & this is my life, & my m^{r}
wch is strange now a dayes^ ⌜is⌝ an honest gentleman y^{t}
neuer inclosd, m^{r} Wellcome of wellcome hall but
[L] pray gentlewoman will yo^{u} sit down & tast.
Con: may ye not from yor sportfull iunketing
Spare me yor meanest shepheard boy y^{t} knowes
The way to m^{r} wellcomes. I will recompence
His paines wth thankfull tender of reward
To make his labour more insensible.
King. If yo^{u} would haue a guid to lead yo^{u} thith^{r}
Ile do't my selfe so please yo^{u}. Goodman Cruch
I pray supply my place yo^{u} ha bene good at it

to come to is interlined at 2406. This revision then cancelled and *in my desires* interlined at 2404; *Is* substituted with caret for *One* at 2407. Revised reading is *yet the selected place in my desires* | *Is m^{r} Wellcomes house.* 2405 *place^*] caret positioned under *ce* 2407 *[One]^*] caret positioned under *ne* 2410 *takepart*] words run together as in MS 2421 *[herald][s]*] *herald* and *s* separately cancelled 2422 *[yo^{u}]^*] caret positioned under *u*

Cruch. Nay *fekins* Ile not leaue ye gentlewoman
Till I see her at the hall.
Con: Old moth^{r} yo^{u}
I hope will take like paines [the k⟨ ⟩]
Old wo: yy mary will I gentlewoman.
Con. I owe a great debt to the king of shepheards
That [such a] ⌜at the⌝ sodaine [sumons of a stranger] ⌜importunitye⌝
⌜Of an vnknown stranger heel be wrought⌝
[Can work him to ye [⌜such a⌝] wondrous reliction] to leaue
[Of] His sport & faire societye.
King: O Lord forsooth it is not so much worth,
Ile be proud to be yor gentle man vsher.
Con: And I a thankfull manifester of
The obligacõn yo^{u} ingage me in
King. Be merry Lads, Ile come againe before
yo^{u} haue [done]‸ ⌜finisht⌝ yor dance, strike musicians
Euery man his wench & mine looke on, Ile
[come againe] make all‸ ⌜the⌝ hast I can, that she
may bestirr her stumps. p^{r}pare Tib. ⌊*Ex. King. Con:*
Cruch. & his wife

[FOL. 132V p. 28V]

Tib. I shall be sory to haue yo^{u} find me vnprouided.
They dance & Tib sits by. After the dance
Enter King of shepheards
King: Thanks louely Tib thy patience shewes thou canst
beare, thy expectation that thou art of a good be=
leefe [like a London taylor,] & thy stay so long in
a place that thou wert not hatcht vnder a lap=
wing; but the cow calfe of a beast that tooke de=
light in one pasture. Come away the next day shall
make vp what we are short in now euery man
to his charge, faire maids we thank yo^{u}, [euery]
[day] [we] ⌜and⌝ hope yo^{u} will‸ ⌜often⌝ make vs more yor debters

2441 *yo^{u}*] mark in MS immediately following shaped somewhat like superscript opening parenthesis 2442 *[the k⟨ ⟩]* words smudged 2445–7 *That … reliction*] original reading: *That such a sodaine sumons of a stranger | Can work him to ye wondrous reliction*; *such a* interlined over cancelled *ye* (2447); *at the* interlined over cancelled *such a* (2445) and *importunitye* interlined over cancelled *sumons … stranger*. *Can … reliction* then cancelled along with interlined *such a*, and *Of an … wrought* interlined (partly over *such a*). Revised passage reads *That at the sodaine importunitye | Of an vnknown stranger heel be wrought.* 2448 *His*] *H* over *h* 2459 *shall*] terminal *l* over *t* 2464 *[like … taylor,]* cancellation mark runs under rather than through the passage 2465 *place*] small squiggle resembling *s* positioned over *e*

theres for yo^{u}. [*Giues the musick mony. Exeunt ōēs*
Enter at the other dore Mr Spruse.
Sp: Mortalls suruiue disasters, that their sense
may know a difference; did we not liue to beare
Mischances, [th'] ⌜the⌝ impartiall hand of fate
were conscious of iniustice; benefitꝭ
Are p^{r}parations to calamitye
And if a man [hat] haue liu'd [to haue a ꝑt] ⌜so happily⌝
[T] [of ioy] ⌜To share in ioy⌝, tis Iustice [that alike]∧ [⌜a⌝] ⌜like⌝ ꝓportion
Of greefe should take possession of his thoughtꝭ
ponding [parity]
[To yeeld a correspo] To make him know how cores=∧ poyse
[Giues Helps]
Giues [stedfast] ⌜euen⌝ motion when the skyes serene
To sayling ships, & ballanceth their great
Vnwieldy bulks in a tempestuous sea.
Should death [attend]∧ ⌜succeed⌝ my wish, the expiration
would taxe my selfe-esteeme, should I deplore
my life, it were less manly then to slight
The troubles y^{t} attend it; he y^{t} bewailes
His being is∧ ⌜not so⌝ [less] meritorious
[Then]∧ ⌜As one⌝ [he] that [scorns] ⌜smiles⌝ at introduced ills.
fe⟨ ⟩ The [one]∧ ⌜last⌝ hath hope, the other in despaire
weeps like a child in such a base deiection
As if thingꝭ [could] were impossible to rise
To any height of mending. Application
names me infected, [a diuersitie] diuersity of wayes
[of wayes to resolution]
To resolution [offered]∧ ⌜[ꝓstitute]⌝ [themselues]∧ ⌜humbly yeeld⌝ themselues
To my disturbed app^{r}hension
And bidd me choose, how [could] ⌜can⌝ I make election
The oracle replyeing doubtfully

2479 *[that … ⌜like⌝]* cancelled *a* positioned above cancelled *that alike*; caret positions interlined *like* 2481 *ponding [parity]*] turned-over line in MS; *poyse* (2482) probably substitution for cancelled *parity* 2487 *[attend]*∧] caret positioned under *en* 2489 *life*] *l* over indiscernible letter 2493 *fe*⟨ ⟩] word only partly formed; might be *feiy* or *feny* *[one]*∧] caret positioned under *e* 2496–9 *Application … yeeld⌝ themselues*] original reading: *Application* | *names me infected, a diuersitie* | *of wayes to resolution*; *a diuersitie … resolution* (2497–8) cancelled and replaced with *diuersity of wayes* | *To resolution offered themselues* (2497 and 2499); *ꝓstitute* interlined for cancelled *offered* then cancelled along with *themselues*; *humbly yeeld* interlined and *themselues* written out again on line 2499 *[themselues]*∧] caret positioned under terminal *s* 2500 *disturbed*] *ed* over *d* 2501 *bidd*] *i* over *a*; terminal *d* over *e*

Or bring oblations to an empty shrine
wth confidence, when I know the S^{t} [was] ⌜is⌝ absent
To whom I owe my pilgrimage? If I die
By mine own hand the action is ignoble

[Fol. 133 p. 29]

29.

And she will haue a seruant fewer. If 133
I liue my life will be vnprofitable
Vnles a[n informacõn] ⌜firm assurance⌝ of her being
In safety make it vsefull. I haue obserud
And ꝓsecuted obseruation
wth such a curious search there's not a tree
In all the forest whose in [closeing]^ ⌜circling⌝ rind
Is capable of an imp^{r}ssion
I haue not bene at councell wth, iust starrs
Beare witnes she cõmanded it, & can
Obseruance suꝑerogate, & soffer
[Suffer for ou^{r}doeing; for I'm sure]
For being too inquisitiuely sedulous?

Enter Crisp.

Better or worse? speake out
Cris: may't please yo^{u} S^{r}.
Sp: I shall be pleased as thy [newes inuites] ⌜short relation⌝
Offers me cause.
Cris: Did you not see the shepheard S^{r}?
Sp: The shepheard! I haue neuer seene a man
Or els thought all men trees since^ ⌜y^{e}⌝ faire queene
Of beauty did inioyne me to examine
⌜[my sight] mine eyes⌝
The [barkes] ⌜barks⌝ of [all] those [I had] should fall vpon
But didst thou see a shepheard?
Cris: yes S^{r}
A shepheard of signification
yor vnckle wellcomes shepheard.
Sp: O hadst thou met
The ministeriall angell [Chariti] ⌜that's⌝ design'd
To wait on Constance, & receiu'd intelligence

2514 *in [closeing]* ^] space between *n* and *c* as in MS; caret positioned under *ei* 2518 *soffer*] *o* over letter that is possibly *a*

From him of her safe being, [twere‸ somw^{t}‸] ⌜it had bene⌝ punctuall.
Cris: Let not my faithfull seruice be [receiu'd] [⌜entertaynd⌝] receiud
wth incredulitye Like Cassandra's councell
And I will raise yor wonder, & outgoe
The [ꝓposition]‸ ⌜supposition⌝ of yor own desire
Sp: Thou strikest me dumbe, my diligent attention
Shall not intrude an interruption
So to ꝓduce‸ ⌜my⌝ [my]‸ [⌜a⌝] satisfaction sooner.
Cris: Then S^{r} beleeue me as yor‸ ⌜knowne⌝ experience
Hath found me euer seruiceable, I met
yor vnckle wellcomes shepheard, coming from
His m^{rs} house, (the place yor selfe intended
To bring yor m^{ris} to[o]), [his p^{r}sent errand] ⌜whither he sayes⌝
He did conduct her safe
Sp: my *Constance* safe!
Cris: As yo^{u} or I. S^{r}, & will there remaine
Vntill the inquiry of a day or two

[Fol. 133v p. 29v]

Do satisfye her whether it be ꝓbable
To heare of yo^{u} or no. yor noble vnckle
Gaue her a wellcome (as his man relates)
Worthy her selfe, & p^{r}sently remitted
His shepheard to a sodayne inquisition
For yo^{u}, I mett the newes & him, sent back
The man vnto his m^{r}, promiseing
To be wthin [a] ⌜a⌝ bow shoot of the place
Yo^{u} now reside in, he likewise gaue his word
To bring his m^{r} hither; as yo^{u} haue bene
A patient bearer of afflictions
Retayne yor vertue still.
Sp: If halfe be true
It is the fayrest morning after rayne
That euer shone vpon [the plowmans labour] ⌜a wearied man⌝.
Cris: If it be false the shepheard is the most
ꝑfidious slaue that euer did conu^{r}se

2539 ⌜*it* ... *bene*⌝] interlined above cancelled *twere somw^{t}* with two carets (one under *we* of *twere*, other under *om* of *somw^{t}*) 2543 *[ꝓposition]*‸] caret positioned under *si* 2546 ⌜*my*⌝ ... *satisfaction*] process of revision: *a* interlined with caret directly above cancelled *my* (caret positioned under *my*); *a* then cancelled and *my* interlined to left of cancelled *a* with caret positioned after *ꝓduce* wth beastꝭ of gentle temper

Enter Mr Wellcome & his shepheard.

Shep. That's [his] ⌜y^{e}⌝ man S^{r}
The gentleman I know not.

Sp: My honour'd vnckle
That wch yor [shepheard] ⌜seruant⌝ vnfolded to my man
Besides my nearer obligacõn
(Needles of repetition) here com̃ands
My duty & my thanks.

Well: My dearest nephew
To giue yo^{u} verball wellcome were to take
[The]∧ ⌜Away the⌝ freedome & ꝓprietie, [yo^{u} haue]
∧ ⌜yo^{u} haue⌝ Where I am master.

Sp: Noble vnckle
my ingagem^{t}ꝭ double, treble it [againe] ⌜so farr⌝
As tell me whether the vertuous Lady yo^{u}
Haue entertaynd doe well, t'anticipate yor question
my mother [is]. do's.

well: I heare it gladly Cosin
And doe requite yo^{u} wth a like relation
Of yor deare m^{ris} wellfare.

Sp: [yo^{u} tell me] ⌜O⌝ S^{r} it is
The onely reall sublunarye good
Next to her selfe & sweet fruition.
And I am blest in heareing it confirmd.
As [I haue] you haue known me oft vnmanerly
Pardon it now [& hasten o^{r} accession] ⌜since my zealous mind⌝
⌜Suffers till I behold her⌝
[Into her p^{r}sence]∧ [So longingly desires her]
⌜[Longꝭ]⌝ ⌜[Is earnest]⌝

well: Cosin the neare degree[s]
[B] of consuanguinitie wch we are in makes me
Carefull of all yor actions, sedulous

2584 *[The]*∧] caret positioned under *Th* 2599–2602 *Pardon ... earnest*] stages of revision are apparently *& hasten o^{r} accession* | *Into her p^{r}sence* cancelled and replaced with *since my zealous mind* | *So longingly desires her*; *So ... her* then cancelled and replaced below the line with *Longꝭ* and *Is earnest* in turn, both of which were cancelled in favour of *Suffers till I behold her*, interlined with caret above *Into ... p^{r}sence* 2605 *actions,*] *s,* over original comma

[Fol. 134 p. 30]

30.

Discretion may not taxe vs [vn] of temerity,
And since o^{r} conference will be more incongruous
Before the Lady satisfy a [demand] p~~t~~ar
[⌜desire⌝] ⌜expect [an answer to] to haue yo^{u} answer⌝
Or two I shall [make] [interrogate yo^{u} of]
⌜[to ho]⌝

Sp: I thank yo^{u} for yor serious admonition 134
[well.] And stand p^{r}par'd to doe it willinglye.
well. Then let yor seruant quit the place, the shepheard
And he may wait o^{r} coming.
Sp: pray let [it] be so [S^{r}]. *~~Exeunt~~ Crisp. & Shepherd*
well: Then tell me Cosin did yo^{u} acquaint yor mother
wth what yo^{u} meant to doe?
Sp: yes truly S^{r}
And she approu'edit as [it] doth appeare
Vnder her [own] hand.
well: Since yor coming from her?
Sp. The date will giue an answer to yor doubt S^{r}.
well. A faire deportm^{t} Cosin know me yor freind
As well as vnckle. No sooner had ye Lady
Entred my house, & ceremonies past
Of decencie & complem^{t}, but she
⌜[interrogatories]⌝⌜interrogatories⌝
Preuented some [interrogations] [few necessary questions]
I meant to offer to her, by desireing
my courteous censure of her strange access;
And wth a blushing modestye inquird,
What sisters nature gaue me how ye first
Was calld, the second, & extended questions
Till she came to particularities
Of what their sons names were, & when [she came] ⌜yor name⌝
[To call yor [mn] name] ⌜Was offerd⌝ to^ ⌜her⌝ memory, she stopt

2610–12 *desire* . . . ⌜*[to ho]*⌝] order in which *desire* and *interrogate* . . . *of* were introduced in place of cancelled *make* unclear; likewise unclear at which stage cancelled *to ho* was substituted 2617 *Exeunt*] bar partly through *Exeunt* seems to be part of box marking stage direction 2621 *approu'edit*] original *d* adjusted to *e*, *d* squeezed in 2622 *[own]*] scribbled out 2629–30 ⌜*interrogatories* . . . *questions*] order in which *interrogatories* and *few* . . . *questions* were introduced in place of cancelled *interrogations* unclear

And askt my wife pray how de call y^{t} gentleman
Letting a sad teare fall to testify
Respect she ought yo^{u}.
Sp: That drop was p^{r}cious
O that I had it in a diamond box
It would eclipse the lustre of the stone
And make it [looke like] ⌜seeme a⌝ counterfet
well. Passion a little ouer (to [omiss] omitt
Th vnnecessary circumstance of night)
She did express vnto my wife in priuat
She knew∧ ⌜you⌝ as a freind, but wisht she might
Inioy yo^{u} as a husband, so yt legalitie
[⌜Did⌝] [⌜make⌝] ⌜would make⌝
[would] [might iustifye] ye circũstances iustyfyable
But did beseech her by ye secret [du] tyes
wch women [make]∧ ⌜haue⌝ in priuate, to retaine
Her wish conceald.
Sp: I beseech yo^{u} S^{r}
Abridge yor long relation, [euery minute] ⌜think yo^{u} were once⌝
Tormented wth ye extasie of loue
Though in a less proportion

[FOL. 134v p. 30v]

Well. I come to yo^{u},
my wife inform'd me, & both [we] o^{r} charitye
Could not but iudge the Lady faultles, till
yor coming at the least, [d] &∧ ⌜so⌝ [did] concluded
Suppose yo^{u} did approue it & gaue testimony
of yor moth^{r} equall likeing, to aduenture
[To] [further [⌜make⌝] or rather further a ꝑposall]
[If yor affection were not dissentanye]
⌜A furtherance to this match the[r] gentlewoman[s]⌝
[To set this match a foot, the modestygoodnes]
Retaining much & yet expressing somwhat
Was worthy obseruation, & her father
Though worthles in respect of parentage
Or any other fayre accomplishm^{t}

2654 *[make]*∧] caret positioned under *a* 2656 *yo^{u}*] *u* over *r* 2666 *further [⌜make⌝]*] *make* interlined above *further*, then cancelled; *further* … *ꝑposall* then also cancelled 2669 *modestygoodnes*] *y* squeezed between *modest* and *goodnes*

That can be calld gentile (thingꝭ wch antiquity
In weaker times did think of, but discretion
Slightꝭ as [poore‸ thingꝭ] ⌜too [light] poore⌝ in fortune,) yet able
To answer all thingꝭ but gentilitye
wth the full hand of opulencye. Now [deare] Cosin
yo^{u} may ꝑceaue how vnconstraynd my loue
Aymd to effect yor good.
Sp: I ho^{r} yo^{u}
⌜not wth answerable seruice to⌝
But [farr below yor noble] [care yo^{u} haue vouchaf'd]
[To] [⌜you⌝] [cast vpon me]‸⌜The care yo^{u} haue of me⌝, & my [poore] designes
Be forward worthy S^{r} in this contriuem^{t}
The fewer dayes of respite yo^{u} admit
⌜impediments⌝
[We are] [The] [least]‸⌜We are the⌝ less obnoxious to [vnlookt for hinderances]
Well. Ile be as forward as yor own desires
Can wish a freind
Sp: Then I beseech yo^{u} S^{r}
Be not offended if wth modest earnestnes
I do implore yo^{u} y^{t} we may attend
[Attend] The purely meriting admired Emperes
[Of my] [admired Emꝑes.]
Of my [conceipt] conceipt
⌜[to cleare the all a]⌝⌜to take of troubleous⌝
well. I stayd [to set things in a forwardnes] interruptions
⌜which might haue done yo^{u} preiudice⌝
[And apt them to conueniencye]‸, but now
The way is fayrely cleard, nor shall delay
Lengthen yor suffering by a longer stay
Fin. Act. 4. *Exeunt*

2676 *poore‸*] caret positioned under *po* ⌜*too … poore*⌝] interlined above *poore‸ thingꝭ* 2681 *I ho^{r} yo^{u}*] curved line clarifies that *not … to* is a revision to line below 2684 *me]‸*] caret positioned under *me* ⌜*The … me*⌝] *The* written in fainter ink than rest of insertion and may have been interlined separately, possibly following the deletion of *farr … noble* in 2683 2688 *[We are]*] cancelled marginal insertion written over *Draw* 2692 *earnestnes*] second *n* over letter that is possibly partly formed *f* or *s* 2694 *The*] *T* over *t* 2697–2700 ⌜*[to cleare … conueniencye*] original reading: *I stayd to set things in a forwardnes | And apt them to conueniencye*; *to set … forwardnes* cancelled; *to … all a* interlined above, cancelled, and replaced with *to take of troubleous*, with *interruptions* positioned on line below (2698); *which … preiudice* interlined above cancelled *And … conueniencye*. Final reading: *I stayd to take of troubleous interruptions | which might haue done yo^{u} preiudice*.

⊥ *Act. 5.*
Enter Mr Thrifty Constable & officers
Peter & Iennet.
Thrif: Officers
Const: S^{r}
1 Off: Here an it please yor wor^{p}.
Thrif: Harnes yor flanders mare, & dispatch the
execution

[Fol. 135 p. 31]

Const: p^{r}sently S^{r}, Bedles geare away. 135 31
Ien: I beseech yo^{u} S^{r} examine fully, whether I were in
fault alone, if I had partners let them suffer wth me
Thrif: After ye sentence is past there is no reuocation, Ile
punish the fact & then examine the busines
Pet. I humbly do beseech yo^{u} S^{r} forgiue
[*Pet:*] [Twas] ⌜'Tis⌝ her first fault S^{r}, & others instigation
Did vrge her to it.
Thrif: [What talkst thou of others]∧ ⌜As I told yo^{u} before⌝, though there be no con=
sideracõn to be had of the ꝑsons yet there is of y^{e}
[ꝑsons]∧⌜men⌝, & thou knowest by my match I am to haue
[a] relation to 'hem all m^{r} *Spruse* [shall] ⌜must⌝ be my son in law
⌜& will mary his sister⌝
Pet: my ill memory betrayes me S^{r} please∧ ⌜you⌝ to signe this
warrant, [tis] for another busines *He looks vpon it*
Thrif: How Thomas such a one seruingman, [7] ⌜seuen⌝ yeares a
Clerk & mistake an addition? *Teares the paꝑ.*
⌜dost abuse thy experience and⌝
[O] Thou [abuser of experience] [dost] discredit thy m^{r} [and]
Ien: [abuse thy expe] [S^{r}] S^{r}
As yo^{u} haue euer found me necessary
forgiue my fault onely ag^{t} yor selfe
Thrif: Woman as I told yo^{u} before, the punishm^{t} of offendo^{r}ꝭ
Is the phisick of a diseasd com̃on wealth, I com̃it
yor body to these men & they shall giue yo^{u} a glister
Peter stay yo^{u} to see wheth^{r} the beast draw grace=
fully. *Exit Thrifty.*
Const: Good m^{ris} Iennet take it not vnkindly, tis vsd at

2704 ⊥] bar to left of *Act* as in MS 2720 *others]*∧] caret positioned under *rs* 2722 *[ꝑsons]*∧] caret positioned under terminal *s* 2730 *Thou*] *T* over *t*

London now besides his wor^{ps} pleasure.

Pet: Deare wife it is but one bout for his wor^{ps} sa=
tisfaction, & another in terro*rem femine ig generis*
a thing [soone done,] ⌜most necessary,⌝ & compound wth yor memory not
to twit‸ ⌜yo^{u},⌝, [&] a q^{r} of an hower ends yor vexation.

Ien: Husband I disclayme thee, neighbours I call
ye all to witnes, besides his want of breeding
his disposition is ill, a fellow of a [very‸ ill life,] ⌜loose conu^{r}sation.⌝
stand by to see yor own flesh derided?

Pet: O wife if I haue ⌜a⌝ wart of my hand that [itcheth]‸ ⌜vexeth me⌝
blame [I]‸ ⌜me⌝ not [that]‸ ⌜if⌝ I make an vnction of pigꝭ
blood, or rubb it wth marigold leaues, till I bring
⌜downe,⌝ [⌜smooth⌝] [⌜rough⌝]
it [euen or] [take away] [the ruffe apparance,] & if
an ill humour thrust out an offensiue bunch of my
forehead, shall I not seare it wth a cauteriseing touch
of correction to take a way the excrescencye? Come
executioners Doe yor office. *They bring out a cart & put her in it.*

Const. Will yo^{u} not haue a vaile forsooth?

[Fol. 135v p. 31v]

Ien. Tis my hard fortune, not my faults haue drawne
This punishm^{t} vpon me, this face had neuer
Reason to be asham'd, & it will still
Outlooke my enuious ꝑsecuto^{r}ꝭ.

Pet. A well chang'd tone
my *Iennet* I admire thee were't not too frequent
for husbands to [implore] ⌜ask⌝ their wiues forgiuenes
I would cry thee m^{r}cye, officers
As yo^{u} loue me vse her kindly. *She drawes the cart ouer the stage.*
Enough my loueing freinds this patient beareing
miseries giues me admirable hope. *She comes out of the cart*

Ien. Of what?

Pet: Onely of amendm^{t} in gr̄all?

Ien: A clerklike hope, a well grounded expectation,

2742 *terrorem*] mixed italic and secretary forms 2744 ⌜*yo^{u}*,⌝,] duplication of punctuation as in MS 2749 *[itcheth]*‸] caret positioned under first *t* 2750 *[that]*‸] caret positioned under terminal *t* 2751–3 *bring ... apparance,*] original reading: *bring | it euen or take away the ruffe apparance*; *smooth* substituted for *take away*; *rough* substituted for *ruffe*; *downe,* substituted for *euen or smooth*; *the rough apparance* cancelled. Revised reading: *bring | it downe,* 2765 *wiues*] *u* over *f*

Ile giue yo^{u} a signe of it. | *Giues him a box oth' eare.* |

Question not my reason, & hold yor hands of
I defye obedience, till I be constraynd. | *Exit* |

Pet: Pry thee feele if my eare do not smart, I meane
if it do not glow, but that I mistooke [my] ⌜the⌝ word
I could haue told yo^{u} it smartꝭ, | *Ex. Bedles wth y^{e} cart.*

Con: She has made it warm least yor blood should
Curdle

Pet: Curdle call ye't? she strooke hard & was in ear=
,, nest man. if my heart were not a p^{r}ty good
,, heart nay a heart of virilitye it could not
abide it, [& the] patience shall haue a reward
& a husband y^{t} will beare shall‸ ⌜be sure to⌝ haue enough
to carry, [he shall be recompenc't, but‸ [⌜how⌝] the]
[cleane contrary‸.] [⌜way.⌝] Come wi me Ile know her
reason though I die for't. | *Exeunt* |

[*Enter M^{ris} mumble, Godfrye &*]
Enter. [*M^{ris} Sophia.*] *wild & Ionye*

wild. The nags in good tune y^{u} sayest.

Iony: He's right S^{r} & wonderfull cleene, I wad the
day ware now S^{r}, there's no feare but danger
of being ta lang keept. | *Enter Crisp in hast.* |

wild. What *Crisp* returnd wth yor aduenture?

Crisp: Not so S^{r} but prety faire for the game. [S^{r}.]

wild. [Wh] Are you yet vpon vncertaintyes?

Crisp: The truth is S^{r} my m^{r} is maryed but [is] not
willing the world should take notice of it
till the old Iustice be appeasd, & to that pur=
pose has dispatched me wth this letter to my
[old] [busines] m^{ris} intreating her if it be possible
to [make] ⌜make⌝ an end of the busines, & get m^{r} Thriftyes
good will

[FOL. 136 p. 32]

wild. Tis very good reason she should, for he has got 32
hers I am sure, & she ꝓtestꝭ the lyeing wth a man
of qualitye hath strangely betterd her heareing. 136

2780 *smart*ꝭ] ꝭ over *e*; *d* immediately following hatched out 2788–9 *he ... way.*⌝]] original reading: *he shall be recompenc't, but the* | *cleane contrary*; *how* and *way* interlined; passage cancelled

Cris: I do not app^{r}hend yo^{u} S^{r}.
wild. m^{r} Thrifty has maryed m^{ris} mumble that's the En=
glish on't, & this being so the reconciliation will
be made wthout opposition.
Crisp: yo^{u} tell me wonders
wild. [Nay] I can tell yo^{u} more for I being now of
the familye, am to take vpon me the ho^{ll} state
too, & yor yong m^{ris} *Sophia* is the woman I am
to venture on,
Crisp. Marriage vpon mariage, tis pity the world
should be vnpeopled, or thing*ẜ* at the best grow
worse for [want of] being not taken in time.
but S^{r} a man trusted cannot be at quiet till he
⌜haue⌝ disburdend himselfe faithfully, & I must needs to
my m^{ris}, wilt please‸ ⌜you⌝ to goe S^{r}?
wild. Iony goe yo^{u} to my taylor tell him the day holds
but my mind is altered for my clokes I will ha
them reach to the knee at least, these last fa=
shiond french clokes are‸ ⌜very⌝ ridiculous, the ape at
the beare garden has one of 'hem they. say.
Iony. I's gang & tell him S^{r}: *Exit*
wild. Now I goe wth thee Dick. *Exeunt*.
[*Enter Mr Strife & Godfrye.*] ⌜*Enter Peter & Iennet*⌝
Pet: Fy wife fye affliction me thinks should ha
wrought a better effect then to strike yor hus=
band before companye.
Ien: And me thinks discretion should haue made yo^{u}
submiss to her y^{t} was yor first rayseing, yo^{u}
cannot deny but from a poore scriueners boy
I aduanced‸ ⌜you⌝ to be yor m^{rs} Clerk, nay yo^{u} are come
to this height, that neuer any man makes
suit to him but he cryes Peter shall I grant
it, & yet now yo^{u} dare [take the] ⌜be so⌝ bold as con=
tend wth yor foundres. To see the vnspeakeable
pride of a [fell] begger on horseback.
Pet. Reuile not yor head.
⌜breed a boy to a man & heel leaue yo^{u} when⌝
Ien. Mary gep pen & inkhorne, [wheres my m^{r}, see]

2846 *breed*] *r* over *e*

⌜yo^{u} ha most need on him, euen my own case but sirrah, sirrah⌝
[ye work him to be pleasd & frown not yo^{u} though]
⌜now yo^{u} haue y^{e} power work yor m^{r} to be pleasd, & frown not though⌝
yo^{u} know certaynly yor wife goes to St Antlins
[⌜or playnly to open thy vnderstanding cuckolds thee⌝]

[FOL. 136v p. 32v]

els as I haue exalted yo^{u}, Ile shew yo^{u} a trick of de=
iection, & make thee repent in teares thou hast
eucr prouok'd me.

Pet: O thou ꝑfect *Xantippe* but that thou wantst a
chamberpot, thou virago, or because I will haue
a word of capacitye to expresse thee Thou woman
& there's enough.

Ien: Sirrha if rep^{r}hension will do no good on yo^{u} bea=
ting shall *Puls out a trunchion* Come of
wth yor hat, & wthout expostulation vsher me
to yor m^{r}, the pride of a buckrom bag is of a
naughty colour

Pet. How a healthfull bodye will be taken downe
wth a disease I quake wthout an ague. *Lets fall her muffe*

Ien Peter my muffe, goe back, Sirrha, I ha lost.
He fetcheth it: & giues it her
What a great comfort a well tutord child
is to his parentꝭ, take me by th' arme, so. *Exeunt*

Enter Mr Strife. & Godfrye.

Strife. As thou hast euer bene vsefull & behoouefull to
me *Godfrye*, so as I am a gentleman I haue euer
giuen thee halfe my fees I receau'd.

Godf. I did what I could S^{r} but 'twas to no purpose.

Strife. Vrge her againe man, & here's the other
halfe crown w^{ch} [I receiued this morning] ⌜in the vacation is a fee⌝
[for putting my hand to a booke.] [⌜bill⌝] ⌜not to be despised⌝

Godf: I will not lye to yo^{u}, S^{r} nor iniure yor expectation
Truly S^{r} my m^{ris} is maryed.

2850 *pleasd*] *p* perhaps written over *h*   2852 *[⌜or … thee⌝]*] revision squeezed onto bottom of page   2854 *iection*] *c* over *f* or *s*   2878–9 *I receiued … despised⌝*] original reading: *I receiued this morning* | *for putting my hand to a booke* [*booke* revised to *bill*]; passage cancelled and *in the vacation is a fee* | *not to be despised* interlined (*not … despised* positioned to left of *bill*)   2880 *yo^{u}*] *u* over *r*

Strife. Out knaue & hast kept me in hand all this while,
I left my Landres vnpayd, & halfe my Comons
last tearme onely to keep touch wth thee, & hast
thou seru'd me so?
Godf: Good S^{r} remember yor selfe did yo^{u} neuer take
a mans fee that his cause went ag^{t} him?
Strife. I can warrant no mans cause.
Godf: Nor I yor success S^{r}, & so good m^{r} Contention m^{r}
Strife I should ha sayd fare ye well S^{r}
Strife. But yet a word more *Godfrye.*
Godf: In peace & quietnes if yo^{u} please, but not a tittle
in passion, I, S^{r}, the lawe's costly.
Strife. Ile express my selfe moderately, nor will I be so
poore as to recall the halfe crowne I last gaue
thee wth a condiconall intention, but onely de=
sire that I may from thy m^{ris} own mouth

[Fol. 137 p. 33]

137 33

receaue my discharge.
Godf: Ile vndertake the Clerk of the parish shall do it
sufficiently, for he setꝭ downe all the mariages wth
his own hand, it may be my m^{r} will take it ill S^{r}, &
yo^{u} know how a man [of] ⌜in⌝ authoritye displeasd may
stick oth' skirtꝭ of a poore seruing creature, I pray
excuse me S^{r}.
Strife. Let my importunitye p^{r}uaile wth thee
Onely to tell her I am here.
Godf: That I will S^{r}, if yo^{u} had not a beard I should think
yo^{u} were a woman yor longing is so violent. *Exit*
Strife. How marrye an ordinarye p^{r}sident guided capon ta=
⌜gentleman in very good practise⌝
king Iustice, & neglect a [bencher] [of] that onely
[out] ⌜in respect of⌝ ꝑsonall desert, & approbation of his knowne
abilities is heard out of course wth fauour at
[⌜a thing seldome done though lately⌝]
most barrs i' the kingdome. It is as ominous
as to [haue] [⌜s⌝] ⌜haue⌝ an Ins of court breake vp com=

2917 *[haue] [⌜s⌝] ⌜haue⌝]* *haue* cancelled, *s* interlined above and cancelled, *haue* interlined to right of cancelled *s*

mons i the‸⌜middle⌝ [middle]‸ of a terme. Merit so vn=
derualued! If women were the imꝑatiue sexe
& might appoint the formalities for all de=
grees & ꝓfessions, I wonder what habitꝭ we
Lawyers should [argue]‸⌜goe to westminster⌝ in. But this haue I
⌜a widow a crackt com̃oditye⌝
for relyeing vpon [fraitye], and ꝑplexing my ⌜selfe⌝
wth an incumbred title wthout a sufficient war=
rantye. *Enter Mr Thrifty m^{ris} mumble [Godfry] Peter & Iennet.*

Thrift: Truly wife though yo^{u} thought it was too much
for yo^{u} to haue a wayting woman in yor widowhood
yet yor place as my wife calls fort as I told yo^{u}
before, & yo^{u} shall haue a competible respect.
m^{r} Strife cry yo^{u} mercy S^{r}, it is my good fortune
S^{r} that hath giuen me more power to bid yo^{u} well=
come here S^{r}, then I [could] ⌜had⌝ wthin this fortnight [S^{r}] [⌜as⌝]
[I told yo^{u} before S^{r},] by two nightꝭ lodging wth the
m^{ris} of the house & all her estate‸⌜to boot⌝, & being inabled
S^{r} as I told yo^{u} before you'r most heartyly well=
come good m^{r} Strife.

Strife. For yor wellcome S^{r} I thank yo^{u}, the ciuill word deserus
no less a recompence, nether come I to giue yor
now house an offence S^{r}, yet a promise made S^{r} will
lye we know that in law, & a promise made vpon a
[valueable]‸⌜valueable⌝ consideracõn S^{r}, is a thing worth prosecuting
& I shall take my opportunitye

[Fol. 137v p. 33v]

Thrif: O S^{r} I take it yor the gentleman othe long robe
that spoild a busines in the handling.

[mũ:] *Strife* [S^{r} I am th] S^{r} I am the man [whom] m^{ris} mumble now
yor wife cannot‸⌜deny⌝ but had interest

mũ: Las good m^{r} Strife, what betweene my deafenes
& my ill memory, I ether mistooke yo^{u} or forgot
yo^{u}, when I am widow againe I will —

2918 *the‸⌜middle⌝ [middle]‸*] *midst* revised to *middle* (*le* over *st*), cancelled, then *middle* interlined with two carets (second caret positioned under first *d* of cancelled *middle*) 2942 *vpon*] *v* over *i* 2943 *[valueable]‸*] caret positioned under *ea* 2947 *[th]*] loop of *h* only partly formed 2948 *Strife*] an s-shaped line links speech prefix to 2947 in place of cancelled *mũ:*

Strife Cry yo^{u} mercy I shall in the meane time make
yo^{u} pay for yor mistakes. *Offers to goe out.*
Thrif: m^{r} Strife a word wth yo^{u} S^{r} to strengthen yor title,
yo^{u} know in law what possession signifies, & liue=
ry & season before giuen & taken, now S^{r} to bee=
uiat yor cause I offer these thingꝭ to yor vnder=
standing, [& councell yo^{u} as a freind] ⌜conceiue of them as⌝ yo^{u} please.
make ready supper S^{r}ꝭ betimes, a fitt of affection
comes vpon me, we new maried folks loue to goe
to bed early m^{r} Strife yor kind freind & riuall S^{r}‸‸ ⌜as I told yo^{u} before⌝.
Strife. So S^{r} abuse vpon abuse yor sufficiency [*Ex: All but Strife.*]
giues the plaintife more incouragem^{t} to goe on,
if I can but light of an Atturnye y^{t}ꝭ [but] as very
a knaue as [this dull]‸ ⌜a⌝ Iustice of peace his Clerk
[is], I shall haue ꝓbability for my paines at least *Exit*
Thrif: *Suo sibi? suo sibi?* how is it Peter?
Peter. *Hunc iugulo gladio* S^{r},
Thrif: Peter I acknowledge thee, it is so indeed Peter
Thou art the ƀre scholler as I told thee before; the
lawyer hath touchd [the] ⌜a⌝ [ill] member of [gou^{r}] ⌜Iustice⌝.
[*Enter*]
Peter. S^{r} He has, but shewd little discretion to slight vs,
yor wor^{p} had done wonderfull well S^{r}, to haue re=
buk'd his carriage, such anoth^{r} halfe howers beha=
uiour makes a contempt, a very palpable one.
Enter M^{r} wild M^{ris} Sophia, & Crisp:
wild. S^{r} heres a messenger come from *Kit Spruse*, wth his
seruice to yo^{u} & a łre to his mother.
Thrif: He do's well freind Richard.
mũ. O how do's kester how do's my boy?
Crisp: If he haue not a countermand he will sodaynly
be here an please yo^{u}. forsooth. I am sure he's ons
way, his m^{ris} m^{r} wellcome [an's] ⌜& his⌝ wife, & more of
good fashion wth him. this łers to yo^{u} forsooth.
Thrif: Is *Constance* but his m^{ris} yet? *She reads.*
Crisp: No ant please yor wor^{p} S^{r}, onely they sit both of a

2953 *Offers ... out.*] box finished with curled brace on right *Offers*] *O* over *S* 2961 ⌜*as ... before*⌝] interlined with two carets 2965 *dull*]‸] caret positioned under *u* 2973 *but shewd*] *but s* partly over cancelled *Enter* at 2972

side ith' coach. [like] and dare not go further wthout
yor wo^{rps} good will

[FOL. 138 p. 34]

Thrif. I here giue it him before witnes as I told yo^{u} before. 34
mũ: Loue pray looke o my †er. 138
wild They sit both of a side ith Coach yo^{u} say?
Cris: yes S^{r}.
Sop: So shall yo^{u} sweet heart for [some] ⌜a⌝ moneth aft^{r} yo^{ur} maried
& then some oth^{r} spruce fashionisht shall haue that place
& yo^{u} ride on horseback ith' rayne
wild. As I ['m vertuous] ⌜loue yo^{u}⌝ I'm i yor debt for that.
mũ. Richard I [a] must referr yo^{u} to my husband for answer,
⌜tis his day of cõmand by couenant of mariage⌝
yet yo^{u} may tell my son this from my selfe that my
deafenes is quite gone wth lyeing wth a man of wo^{rp}:
Thrif: Freind [Spruse] ⌜*Crisp*⌝ tell yor m^{r} in breefe that as I told yo^{u}
before he shall be wellcome, & that his hast in his
[busines] ⌜mariage⌝ has giuen me no offence.
Crisp: yor wor$^{p[s]}$ good health S^{r}. ⌊*Exit.*
wild. Now my day I beseech yo^{u} S^{r}.
mũ. What sayes *Sophia*?
Sop: my phisician has assurd me I can take no hurt
at these yeares forsooth, but I had rather [take] ⌜relye vpon⌝ yo^{u} for
aduise that haue tryed. [forsooth.]
Thrif: Daughter for so now you'l giue me leaue to call yo^{u}
⌜yo^{u} may take his securitye⌝
yo^{u} vrge it well‸ [he] that knowes yor constitution, [so]
[well] he's warrant sufficient.
wild. Then let me begg this reall fauour from yo^{u},
[The day may be electiue & set downe]
[By my deare m^{ris} selfe dispose]
That since no dayes peculiar circũstance
Can hinder ⌜it⌝ from being eligible
But an vnlookt for accident (wch starrs
Of good portent detayne,) yor ioyned sufferance
will giue my m^{ris} liberty to choose
The night wherein she must sustaine a loss

2998 *[a]*] *a* leads into first turn of *m* or *n* 3009 *yo^{u}*] *u* over *r*

will make her smile to beare.

mum. Let 'hem take their own time good loue.

Thrif: Sweet m^{r} wild as I told yo^{u} before S^{r}, be it known to yo^{u} & all people, as I am bound by my place to be a pacificall reconciler of differences so I [wth y^{e}] desire yo^{u} may ioyne wth all conuenient expedition, ⌜the choice of the time⌝ & leave‸ [it] to yor selfe S^{r}, & yor dayntye deare yor thankꝭ S^{r} I expect in [yor] ⌜the wedding⌝ gloues as I told yo^{u} before.

Sop: They shall fit yor hand Sr Ile pass my word.

Thrif: And [Ile beleeue] as I told yo^{u} before Ile rely more vpon‸ ⌜y^{t}⌝ securitye, then a Lords oath or a k^{t}ꝭ bond my little nightingale

[Fol. 138v p. 34v]

Sop: I hope wthin a yeare to haue a child Shall wth a smile express the moth^{r}ꝭ thankꝭ.

Pet: And now S^{r} at the latter end of a day, I beseech yor fauour to yor old seruant *Peter*, for since I ꝑformd yor cōmand to see Iustice done vpon this feminine siñer *Turns to Iennet* she has baffelld me as if I were one of her charr women.

Thrif: *Peter* you mistake Iustice is done, the party cleard, sa=tisfaction giuen yor wife set at libertie as I told yo^{u} before

wild. my fellow sufferer accused?

Ien. S^{r} I beseech yo^{u} heare me, this fellow that for res=pectꝭ known to yor wo^{rp} I ⌜haue long⌝ vouchafed to call husband is of a very ill life, he's ꝓfuse at the alehouse a niggard to me, spends all abroad, yet denyes me necessary cherishing though I demand it, & then all his fence is Iennet I cannot doe as I haue done, & S^{r} I hope when thingꝭ are brought [af] before yo^{u}, you'l rather incline to fauour the weake, then vphold the refractorye, [S^{r}] all my neighbo^{r}ꝭ know since yor wo^{rps} fauour has bene wthheld, I was in great danger of being chapfalln, I haue lookt wan & thin; S^{r} his imꝑfections are knowne, his dis=ability of body diuulgd, & but that I would not haue

3031 *yor selfe*] small squiggle just to left of superscript *r* letter not fully formed 3048 *vouchafed to*] *d* squeezed in 3053 *af*] *f* uncertain;

yor displesure a good lusty brawny collier deserues
a woman [before] ⌜better then⌝ such a meager rascall, & should
haue inioyed me before the picture of Lent in
round trunks, but yor wor^{p}full word had power to
com̃and & shall euer [S^{r}]. wth me [S^{r}].

Thrif: Wife she shall be thy waiting woman, a french
gown & a roll will make her [competible]‸⌜complete⌝.

Peter. And what shall I do I beseech yo^{u} S^{r}?

Ien: mary get a pen that writes fuller sweet husband
⌜& not scrible scrable like a boy that [writes]⌝⌜runs crooked⌝
[all y^{t} yo^{u} can doe is but to scrible scrable, & write]
⌜[crook'd], though his booke, be ruld wth two lines⌝
[a hand y^{t} nobody can reade.] get me a text pen
⌜I say againe that writes fuller,⌝
‸ make yor words legible, & neuer [mak] draw a
stroke but cry wife do's it please yo^{u}? merit ex=
pect℮ obseruance, & one y^{t} has bene well fed by her
m^{r} will not be starud by his man, yo^{u} [sh] must be indus=
trious, or know Ile renounce thee wth shame.

mũ. How well mirth does between husband & wife.

Thrif: Admirable well wife as I told yo^{u} before, come come
shake hands yo^{u} loueing couple, yo^{u} express passion
but haue none, shew anger yet neuer knew it, red=
⌜[& follow] the phi⌝
den onely to make yor blood thin [ad ruborem non]
sicians

[FOL. 139 p. 35]

139 35

rule‸ ⌜good,⌝ *Ad ruborem*‸ ⌜*tantũ.*⌝, [*non ad sudorem,*] where suspition has bene
conceiu'd let it die, if a fault ha bene com̃itted [bef] beleefe
[is]‸ ⌜shall be⌝ most officious to think it none. Two mariages haue
⌜m^{r} wild & yor daughter wife are⌝
bene [these two are]‸ like to make [those three]‸ ⌜the third⌝, besides yo^{u}

3064 *[S^{r}]*] second *S^{r}* may not be cancelled; thin line that looks like cancellation mark may have been made by pen dragging through *S* to form superscript letter 3066 *[competible]*‸] caret positioned under *m* 3069–74 ⌜*& not … legible*] original reading: *all y^{t} yo^{u} can doe is but to scrible scrable, & write | a hand y^{t} nobody can reade. | make yor words legible.* Revised version: *& not scrible scrable like a boy that writes | crook'd* [revised to *runs crooked* |], *though his booke, be ruld wth two lines | get me a text pen | I say againe that writes fuller, | make yor words legible.* 3077 *[sh]*] *h* only partly formed 3085 *sicians*] positioned as in original 3089–91 *Two … those*] inked line links *T* of *Two* in 3089 to *t* of *those* in 3091 3091 *three]*‸] caret positioned under *ee*

Peter & Iennet shall be new maried‸⌜ouer againe⌝. when my son ⌜*spruse*⌝ &
daughter come home, [the first] ⌜the first⌝ night [w the]‸⌜we⌝ three marie⟨d⟩
⌜Peter & Iennet⌝
couples [shall] ⌜will⌝ lye all in a chamber‸⌜togeth^{r},⌝, & yo^{u} two‸ in the truc=
kle bed as I told yo^{u} before, sack possetꝭ shall goe a beg=
ging, & his wife that frownes next morning shall relate
the cause, or els haue the greatest punishm^{t} inflicted y^{t}
[⌜a dayes silence at the whole⌝]
a woman can be designed to, [& that is be inioynd]‸ [a days]
[to hold her tong.] [⌜next gossiping.⌝] [*Enter Godfrye.*]

mum: whats that deare husband.

[*Godf.* S^{r} an please yo^{u} according to yor appointm^{t} I haue from] [⌜staid vpon⌝]

⌜*Pet.* without question forsooth for a she ward to be mari=⌝
[the top of the house, & thence discou^{r}ed the company]
⌜ed, & then of the sodayne be taken from her husband before⌝
[I think yo^{u} looke for]
⌜she [can] has [lost]‸⌜time to loose⌝ her maidenhead.⌝

[*Thrif:* Letꝭ in that vpon o^{r} return as I told yo^{u} before, o^{r} coming]

⌜*Ien:* To see the continued impudence of an vnmanerly *Clerke*⌝
[may be receaued wth the more acceptance & o^{r} salutacõns]
⌜take the answer out of his m^{rs} worp^{full} mouth,.⌝
[appeare more gracefull to the spectato^{r}ꝭ. *Exeunt*.]

Thrif: O thou experience tryed *Iennet* how tender is thy sence
of my venerable reputation, deliuer thy selfe oracu=
lously what is in thy opinion a womans greatest vexa=
tion?

Ien: O S^{r} truth cannot lye though it weepe for't, nor may‸⌜we⌝
conceale those greefes that wring vs when a man
of wo^{rp} doth examine; but my woes too truly tell

3093 *[w the]*‸] caret positioned under *t* *marie⟨d⟩*] edge of page has flaked away; only left-leaning loop of *d* still visible
3095 ⌜*togeth^{r},*⌝,] duplication of punctuation as in MS 3099–3101 *a dayes . . . tong*] Original reading: *& that is be inioynd a days* | *to hold her tong*. Penstroke cancelling *& . . . inioynd* extends under *a days*; *a days* scored through with a second pen-stroke, suggesting it may have been cancelled separately. Revised reading: *& that is be inioynd a dayes silence at the whole* | *next gossiping*. Context suggests *day* adjusted to *days* before phrase cancelled; *ys* of *days* visible on brittle folded-back fragment of page. 3101–13 *[Enter . . . Exeunt.]* Godfrey's appearance revised out. Original reading: *Godf. S^{r} an please yo^{u} according to yor appointm^{t} I haue from* [*from* revised to *staid vpon*] | *the top of the house, & thence discou^{r}ed the company* | *I think yo^{u} looke for* | *Thrif: Letꝭ in that vpon o^{r} return as I told yo^{u} before, o^{r} coming* | *may be receaued wth the more acceptance & o^{r} salutacõns* | *appeare more gracefull to the spectato^{r}ꝭ. Exeunt*. Revised reading: *Pet. without question forsooth for a she ward to be mari=* | *ed, & then of the sodayne be taken from her husband before* | *she can* [*can* revised to *has*] *lost* [revised to *time to loose*] *her maidenhead.* | *Ien: To see the continued impudence of an vnmanerly Clerke* | *take the answer out of his m^{rs} worp^{full} mouth,.*

me S^{r} a man that talks before he is maried, & cheatꝭ
his wife after wth a non ꝑformance S^{r}, & this is the miserie of my poore distressed estate.

Pet: Will yor wor^{p} haue me suffer this to?

Thrif: Vnderstand me *Peter* as I told yo^{u} before, yor patience is
now most congruous, since y^{e} [question]^ ⌜[admin] intergatorie⌝ was administrd
by yor m^{ris}, & so what yor wife sayd came in as a coinci=
dent as I told yo^{u} before & not participating of the
body of the busines as yo^{u} erroneously conceit it, but
since opinion stands variously weele haue youth to goe
vpon it too, m^{r} wild how doe yo^{u} app^{r}hend it.

mum: Very well put husband, very well put.

wild. I am so farr from iniuring the goodnes
That liues in woman, I shall beseech yor fauour
To spare my disability from giueing
A positiue answer.

mum: A dish of maners in a mess of dissimulation
Do yo^{u} know nothing yo^{u} think would vexe a woman?

wild. I hope I neuer shall; but I remember
I saw a Lady angry once because
A gentleman commended her for being

[FOL. 139v p. 35v]

Extremly faire when her tand skin did witnes
His flattery told a lye, or his abuse
Ger'd her on purpose.

Thrif: m^{r} Wild as I told yo^{u} before S^{r} yo^{u} lye of like a spaniell
for a long wing'd hawke, or a setter that dare not goe
neare[r] for feare of springing, weel spare yo^{u} till yo^{u}
be in the honest mans row, & then pitty yo^{u} if ye dare
not deliu^{r} yor mind.

mũ: Nay then Ile haue *Sophia* speake.

Sop: No pray forsooth.

mũ. yo^{u} shall not say me nay, speake out thou knowst
what women will take pet at

Sop: [I haue no cause] Not I forsooth
And if heauen please to shine on m^{r} wild
wth charitable lustre, I shall hope [to die]

3126 *[question]^*] caret positioned under *n*

To liue vntaken notice of by sorrow
And die wthout an interuening cause
To shed a teare

Thrif: A well mett couple may yor first child proue a wise
⌜the prouerb needs no commentary⌝
man‸ ⌜truly⌝, I [doubt] ⌜feare⌝ it, [yo^{u} being past one and twenty],
but because doubts are rais'd, they must be cleared,
& it were a great detraction from the sufficiency
of a man in place, to heare a busines confusd or
many things iumbled together, wch he by learnd di=
uision or a [contrary] ⌜coniunctiue⌝ dispose [he] could not in a trice
make ether *Continua Quantitas* or *discreta*‸ ⌜at plesure⌝ [as I told]
[yo^{u} before]. Therefore in this one particular Ile shew
my iudgem^{t}, & make it appeare to yo^{u} as cleare as the
[⌜the⌝] Sun, or the king(armes in the Shire hall, that the
greatest punishm^{t} [can] ⌜can⌝ be inflicted vpon a woman
is to be inioynd a whole dayes silence at a gossip=
ping, thus haue I opend the cause, giuen a satisfac=
tory answer & yo^{u} must all confess transcended farr
those [‸] inferiour capacities‸ ⌜& humile vnderstandings⌝ that interpret law the
wrong way, & ꝑuert the [meaneing] ⌜intention⌝ of a statute
[onely] to [serue their own corrupt purposes]‸ ⌜[or] mislead a iurye⌝ [as I]
[told yo^{u} before]. *Enter Godfrye.*

Godf: S^{r} I haue according to yor direction attended vpon the
leads, & euen now discouerd ye company I think yo^{u}
expect.

Thrif: Family let(away, the more state wee keep, the more
obseruance we attract, & though we are not proud
we will not be cōmon nor vouchafe familiarity
wthout sollicitation as I told yo^{u} before. *Exeunt.*

Enter M^{r} wellcome, M^{ris} wellcome, Mr Spruse
M^{ris} Constance, Crisp, Cruch, & his wife.

Sp: What satisfaction can yor ⌜iournye⌝ giue [me *Crisp*]
my doubfull thought(?

3161 *the ... commentary*] interlineation marked off with partial box 3176 ⌜*&* ... *vnderstandings*⌝] caret before *inferiour* cancelled and phrase repositioned with second caret after *capacities*; thin line drawn from terminal *s* of *vnderstandings* to second caret reinforces revised placement 3186 *Exeunt.*] right-hand side of box finished with a curly bracket 3187 *M^{ris}*] *M* over italic *S* 3189–90 *What ... thought(?*] Original reading: *What satisfaction can yo^{u}* [*u* blotted] *giue me Crisp*. Revised reading: *What satisfaction can yor* [*r* positioned beneath blot] *iournye giue* | *my doubfull thought(?*; 3190 squeezed onto bottom of page

[FOL. 140 p. 36]

Crisp: Thingꝭ goe rarely well S^{r}, yet the newes is strange 36.
both in the town & countrye, for I heare, that soldiers
are led by gownemen, & pikes & musketiers make a re= 140
treat from bickbatꝭ, fleetstreet is become mile end
& more fields a bleching place, barbers haue their
mustachioes turnd vp by y^{eir} m^{rs}, & Iockies their
stirrups held by y^{eir} Lords, Iustice Thrifty$_{\wedge}$⌜has⌝ maried yor
moth^{r} S^{r}, & sweares as he is a man put in trust wth a
diuision, he was neuer angry, & yo^{u} shall be as well=
come to him, as muscadine after brawn or sack be=
fore supper;.

Sp: And how do's he confirme it?

⌜told me before⌝
Crisp: Vpon his wo:^{rpfull}$_{\wedge}$word$_{\wedge}$⌜he said⌝, & as he [is y^{e} Kings leige *Iustice.*]

m^{ris} well: Nay then yo^{u} are well enough nephew, he delights in that
ꝓtestation as much as in sending a fellow to the iayle.

well: And how did my sister take the [soddaine] ⌜sodayne⌝ newes?

Crisp: She laught [when] ⌜as⌝ she [did] read the letter S^{r},
& euery second word that past betweene m^{r} Thrifty
& her selfe, was heark yo^{u} loue, or pray sweet heart
obserue, they play like conies, & toy as if they were
but comeing to y^{t}, [forty] ⌜wch twenty⌝ yeares agoe they were abridgd
of by imꝑfections of vnable bodies

Sp: may it but turn to my aduantage, &
I shall applaud wth voluntary suffrage
Those toyingꝭ wch their liberall conceipt
[But long since] ⌜Is plenteous in but⌝ worn abilityes
Constraynedly forbeare, & be as ioyfull
As their sence seemes delighted.

well: Loose not a iot.
Of time wherein so faire an opportunitye
Inclines wth obuious steps to giue yo^{u} meeting
[Send yor man in,]

Sp: I am ingag'd to serue yor strict comãnds
much more yor councell, whose industrious vigilance

3193 *140*] archivist's page number fitted in above *make a*   3194 *bickbatꝭ*] *sic*   3200 *muscadine*] *d* over letter that is possibly *t*   3204 *wo:^{rpfull}$_{\wedge}$*] *rpfull* squeezed in; caret positioned under *f*   3207 *[soddaine]*] heavily scored out   3215 *shall*] *sa'* apparently adjusted to *shall* (*h* over *a*, *a* positioned under apostrophe)   3218 *ioyfull*] *y* over *u*

Hath thus farr crownd me, nor shall lazye negligence
Render me careles ether to ꝓsecute
Or speake occasion faire, by whose assistance
my [feare]∧⌜doubt⌝ benum̃ed [hopes]⌜feares⌝, [haue] but now enliud
wth the warm blood of hope may be sublim'd
To height & ripenes. Officious *Crisp*, [Be bold] Goe in
[To]⌜And⌝ tell my moth^{r}ꝭ husband m^{r} Thriftye
(I dare not know him by a nearer epithet
Till his faire leaue giue licence) I am come
To clayme his promise & wth thankfull boldnes
Send him my humble seruice. If by chance
yo^{u} see my mother, & a question fall
From her [of] [how I]⌜how⌝ assiduitye of being
A married man becomes me yo^{u} may answer

[FOL. 140v p. 36v]

As absolute ꝑfection as mortalitie
Euer possest to make the labours of
This life seeme easy & a recreation
I haue to make my suffering light; And since
[A]⌜One⌝ word cannot express my happines
Nor her that brings it, I am forc't to vse
[A periphrasis] (To help this imꝑfection) a periphrasis
Or els she must be wrong'd, whose iniury
Is mortall to my app^{r}hension
And I disclayme.
Crisp: This is yor plesure S^{r}?
Sp: This I desire thou mayst haue memory
To [store] keep[e] vntill an apt occasion
Inuite it from thee, quit the place & make
Conuenient hast.∧⌜⌊*Ex: Crisp.*⌝ What muse yo^{u} on my deare?
Con: To think how strange vnlookt for instrum^{t}ꝭ
Ruld by [a]∧⌜the hand of⌝ high contriuem^{t} [haue abilitye] doe
Sometimes beyond hope & the rules we haue
For [probabilytye]⌜likelihood⌝, miraculously rectifye
O^{r} own conceipted steps, the confidence
whereof would lead vs wrong, should we not be

3229 *benum̃ed*] second *e* squeezed in 3246 *To*] *T* over *t* 3252 *[store]*] heavily cancelled; reading uncertain *keep[e]*] *e* heavily blotted and reading uncertain; small blot or mark just below blotted *e*

Reduc'd by heauen, & [these]^ ⌜those⌝ meaner helps
Before we erre too farr. Doe but obserue
O^{r} [bur] birth & selfe esteeme, the iollitye
we got into the coach wth, [the va] o^{r} disiunction
By strange disaster, the sodayne comfort w^{ch},
I cutt ye other circumstances of, [w^{ch}]
To come the sooner to. wonder is poore
To be imploy'd in meditating on
These strange occurrences.
Spr: When yo^{u} are fifty loue
Then exercise yor thoughts in contemplation
you'l haue more time & less to trouble yo^{u}.
m^{ris} well. Thanks for y^{t} nephew
well. Beare wth his [ouerioy] being ou^{r}ioy'd, the m^{r}chant
That getꝭ his ship to land, at least the goods
for wch the seruice, of the ship is valued
Cannot be sad [on] ⌜a'⌝ [flat] [shoare] shore.
Sp: my thoughts obey yo^{u}
Being bound by nearenes of allyance to it.
Con: And I yo^{u} husband, but my thankfullnes
Cannot expire & I suruiue; nor may we
forget that good old man, whose paynfull trauayle
Stands yet vnrecompenc'd, how do yo^{u} father *Cruch*?
Cruch. Limp after the progress, [lik] a little foundred still.
Con: And how do yo^{u} old mother?
Old. wo: I was vp betimes & am a little sleepy now, doe yo^{u} not
vse to bayt, in a whole dayes iournye, pray is't not the
fashion to say a body is not weary when she is, or will
being weary make one a gentlewoman, [if it will not, I]
[⌜cuck stoole⌝]
[⌜these rocking cradles⌝]
[do hence forth defye a coach as much as a cuck^ stoole.]
[are vnwhollsome vpon stones.]

3261 *[these]^*] caret positioned under terminal *e* *meaner*] two small marks resembling an imperfectly formed caret under *r* 3265 *w^{ch}*] reading uncertain; perhaps *wth* 3289–93 *if it ... stones.*] Original reading is *if it will not, I* | *do hence forth defye a coach as much as a cuck stoole*. It seems *these rocking cradles* | *are vnwhollsome vpon stones* was interlined in place of *as much ... cuck stoole*; *cuck stoole* was then interlined above *these ... cradles* (perhaps to produce *these cuck stoole* | *are vnwhollsome vpon stones*?). Passage and revisions were finally all cancelled. 3292 *cuck^*] caret positioned under *uc* 3293 *[are ... stones.]*] positioned as in MS

[FOL. 141 p. 37]

Enter Mr Thrifty, m^{ris} mumble, m^{r} wild, m^{ris} So=
phia Peter Iennet, & Godfrye, 4 country [peo=]
[ple] ⌜men &⌝ women wth p^{r}sents.

Thrif: Peter. 141
Peter. Here S^{r}
Thrif: Put the busines in a forwardnes as I told yo^{u}
before, that my complet[at] salutation may bid y^{e}
strangers wellcome, & as the course is when yo^{u}
haue concluded the matter then ask what my ple=
sure is in the busines.
Peter. I shall S^{r}, come good folks attend, yor name [&] busi=
nes & abiding place | *Thrifty goes toward his strangers.*
Country mã I an it shall like yor good wo^{rp} m^{r} Parchm^{t}.
Peter. Fy fy speake softly. | *The country folks whisꝑ & Peter writes*
Thrifty. A prime part of magistracy as I told you before
consistꝭ [I] in laying by passion, & disclayming parti=
alitye, yet there are many cautions to be obserud
in vouchafeing clementy, to the penitent, & exten=
ding seuerity to the incorrigible & refractory,
now obserue yo^{u} me *consideratis considerandis* &
as I told yo^{u} before your all most heartily well=
come, brother sister son daughter, wth all the imple=
m^{t}ꝭ accoutrem^{t}ꝭ & necessary dependences of yor long
tayld trayne. | *He salutes y^{em} & kisseth the women*
Sp: Except my bold aduenture hath wthdrawn
yor fauour from [vs] these noble furtherers
Of my designes, they may wth rightfull clayme
Challenge yor loue.
Thrif: O S^{r} as I told yo^{u} before I being sworn to keep‸ ⌜the⌝
peace to the best of my power should [be forsworn] ⌜break my oath⌝
if I should nourish malice in my brest, especi=
ally ag^{t} those that are made of my kinred by the
coniunctiue work of matrimonye, I, I say again
be forsworn, euidently forsworn, & yo^{u} must obserue

3297 *141*] no page number marked 3300 *complet[at]*] *t* squeezed between *e* and cancelled *at* to alter *compleat* to *complet* 3305 *strangers.*] full-stop shaped like a very short line with a slight dip in the middle, slightly resembling a dash; pen probably dragged 3314 *consideratis*] a mix of italic and secretary forms 3320 *[vs]*] heavily scored out

as I told yo^{u} before we are neuer to be forsworn
except it be in matters of mom^{t} or busines of
small consequence

Sp: I will not p^{r}ss the rules [th] wch Iustice gouerns by
But thankfully acknowledge yo^{u} vouchafe
The beauteous outside yor Iudiciall robe
Denyes to [me] guilty men, whose sad reuerse
Prophetically speakes their condemnation.

Thrif: O S^{r} condemne, I acquit yo^{u} as I am right wor^{p}full

[FOL. 141V p. 37V]

my noble freinds please yor [selfe]^ ⌜selues⌝ wth discourse
of yor own finding, the country attends, & dex=
terity in expedition wch I am famous for, gets
the good will of a mans ⌜neighbo^{r}ꝭ⌝, & sometimes as I
may tell yo^{u} in priuat a dish of chickins, or
the like, wch are good country prouisions
now corne is so deare. *Thrifty turns frõ thẽ to the suiters.*

m^{r} well. S^{r} we shall attend yor plesure, & gladly
shorten the time wth discourse of thing[ꝭ],
done many yeares agoe; sister this macth
Hath a successfull happines

Thrif: I shall desire yo^{u} as I told yo^{u} before to speake
low my louing broth^{r}, for the^ ⌜comon⌝ peoples obseruati=
on is too apt to be ledd away, & their attention
is most necessary by reason of the diuersity
of [thingꝭ] ⌜heads⌝ wch I am to [handle] ⌜speake vpon⌝, & their dullnes
of app^{r}hension

m^{r} well. I cry yo^{u} mercy S^{r}.

Thrift: Now Peter yo^{u} know I am to take where yo^{u}
leaue, therefore express thy conceipt, & inform
me how farr yo^{u} haue waded into the busines.

Pet: Ant shall please yo^{u} S^{r} for yor better vnder=
standing, & yor more orderly proceeding, here
is a breefe of the busines expressiue & direc=
tory.

Thrif: To wch party doth this busines belong?

3347 *thing[ꝭ]* cancellation of brevigraph uncertain   3348 *macth*] *sic*   3358 *conceipt,*] *pt,* over *t,*

Pet: I haue accom̃odated their busines to y^{e} persons
And placd their [busin] suit(in [the] yor wo^{ps} paper as
they stand in order before yo^{u}.
Thrif: O thou necessary epitomiser of tediousnes, how
most auxiliar thou art to a man perturbd wth
multiplicity of affaires, I conceiue thee to my
own aduantage, & approue thy sufficiency, as
I told thee before.
Pet: S^{r} an it like yor good wor^{p}, these∧⌜two⌝ brought yo^{u} the
p^{r}sent(
Thrif: We must not take notice of that∧⌜openly⌝, but manifest
o^{r} acceptation by fauouring the partyes, & expedi=
tion according to their own desires, but this is
misterium authoritatis∧ [⌜*Peter*⌝] & so vnderstand it. *This he speaks aside.*
Then thus *Peter*, [point(] *Points to y^{e} paper & then to the [men] parties.*
Peter: miraculously app^{r}hended S^{r}
as I perceaue [yor intention of] ⌜yor⌝ sentence intends to
be punctuall.

[FOL. 142 p. 38]

38.

Thrif: The indictm^{t} ag^{t} yo^{u} shall not be found, yor recognizance
taken of the file, yo^{u} sell ale still, & yor daughter escap⟨e⟩
whipping, & yet the parish keep the child, where it
was nether got nor born. 142
1.Coun.wo: Bless yor good wor^{p}, a poore p^{r}sent for yor wor^{p}
Thrif: 'Las neighbo^{r}(, I neuer take bribes,∧⌜but⌝ because yo^{u} shall
not take it vnkindly Ile accept yor good will
1 Coun: wo: mine are but foure chickens forsooth, but should haue
bene fiue, if the fift[h] had not run a way, & I wan=
ted company to catch it. I hope it may be a hen
in time & a damm of more chickens for yor worp^{s}
table.
Thrif: Run a way do yo^{u} say, the fift chicken run away?
1 Cou.wo. yes ant please yo^{u} to my greefe but my good will
was not wanting to shew my thankfullnes to yor
wor^{p}.
Thrif: Nay if that be a hinderance Ile send a man or two to

3366 *[the]*] *e* partly formed 3368 *Thrif:*] *Thr* over *Pet.* *epitomiser*] *r* over *s* 3373 ⌜*two*⌝] *t* over *2*
3378 *[⌜Peter⌝]*] heavily smudged out; reading uncertain 3385 *escap⟨e⟩*] terminal letter partly trimmed

help to catch that extrauigant chicken, that chic=
ken that respectꝭ not authority, & onely for yor repu=
tation that are the giuer, & not my comodity y^{t}
am the receauer as I told yo^{u} before, I would be loth
yor gift should be but fowre, when yor meaning was
fiue, or [kn] haue yor p^{r}sent niggardly, when yor mind
is bountifull

1 Coun. wo At yor wor^{ps} good plesure.

2 Co: wo A couple of fat capons for yor wor^{p}, they are cleane
capons as yor wor^{p} may ꝑceaue by the length of
their tayles

Thrif: Truly neighbo^{r}ꝭ as I told yo^{u} before, I am sory it is
my hard chance to be of so famous a merit, as to
extract out of small proportions such a [large quan]
[titye] ⌜number⌝ of gratuityes,

1 Cou.Man. The country is happy in yor wor^{ps} neighbo^{r}hood.

Thrif: That we vnderstand as I told yo^{u} before, & shall neuer
be willing to hide those partꝭ, wch nature & art [hath] ⌜haue⌝
bestowd to the benefit of ye republique, [neighbo^{r}ꝭ yo^{u}]
[know my dwelling,] Peter yo^{u} see my strangers expect
my return haue my neighbo^{r}ꝭ to the buttry, to my
little buttry ith' parlo^{r}.

All: Long life to the founder. *Exeunt Country folks & Peter*

Thrif: my noble freinds, let not I beseech yo^{u} the life of a
Iustice of peace be had in contempt, who is thus forct
to descend to keepe order in a county, nor do yo^{u} think
erroneously my proceedingꝭ are p^{r}posterous, when my
own abilityes tell me they are regular & immaculate
for euer while yo^{u} liue *primo de* [*priuatis*] ⌜*publicis*⌝ *secundo de pri=
uatis*, in the first place the forrayne in the second the
domestick as I told yo^{u} before

[Fol. 142v p. 38v]

wild. I take y^{e} boldnes in the name of these
yor noble visitantꝭ, to confess they think
Their wellcome as yor free intention
[procla] will haue it, noble. [And takeing] [⌜wth this⌝]

3413 *famous*] Osborne *s* 3416 *The ... neighbo^{r}hood*] speech indented as in MS 3434 *think*] *t* over *c*

[wth generall consent] And because I am
[we] vrgd by mine own concerns, thus out of course
To rayse my probability to height
Of a fruition, I beseech yo^{u} S^{r}
Pardon a yong man earnest, whose extreme
Is but a temperat mediocritye
weighing y^{e} gale he sayles wth in the ballance
Of app^{r}hensiue meditation.
Thrif: m^{r} Wild noble m^{r} wild yor day of mariage S^{r} as
I take it lyes still in yor mind, as I wish my corpo=
ration may neuer be constraynd to creep through
a little wicket, I gaue yo^{u} free licence to choose
yor own day S^{r}
⌜yor faire leaue giuen irreuocable vowes⌝
wild. [The internall was firmly tyed by] [tyes]
Tyed the internall knot, but sensible
Of the defect a ceremonye hath
wch is not grac'd wth store of lookers on
we did [restrayn that liberty vntill] ⌜restrayn the outward complem^{t}⌝
Of mariage till the dayes solemnitye
might be grac'd wth the p^{r}sence of yor freinds
Whose wisht return renders vs sensible
how greeud their absence was. And now beseech yo^{u}
to make yor plesure known.
Thrif: How are those men blest that haue but the discerne
to know desert from merit, & that can giue an aw=
full respect to magistracye, when that reuerence
comes home wth a duck ithe mouth as I will now
make it appeare to yo^{u}. Had m^{r} wild my now all=
most son in law huffled for his m^{ris}, I had by my
place caused the contempt to haue bene recorded
& proceeded in discretion. [when] ⌜But⌝ now I must goe
on cleane contrary & in a Iudiciall way send [for]
a warrant for all my neighbo^{r}ꝭ to come to his wed=
ding, wch must be sodayne, & were it not that yo^{u}
Haue bene so long deteynd wth looking on

3450–1 ⌜*yor* . . . *tyes*] the revision to cancelled *The* . . . *by* is probably *yor faire leaue giuen irreuocable tyes*, with *tyes* positioned on the line; *tyes* then cancelled and *vowes* interlined above 3456 *till*] *i* over *l* 3457 *freinds*] *r* over *e*

The progress to this end we should intreat
yor p^{r}sence at the mariage, wch will be
Complet in all thing(but yor company. | *Exeunt* |

Finis

[Fol. 143 p. 39]

Epilogue. 143

So great things end; the maiestie of King(
Hath not aduantage of inferiour thing(
But in the glorious way to ruine, all
The pomp of a maiestick funerall
Being but obliuions prologue. Can a play
But of two howers life suruiue those gay
Adorned high built tropheies? Poetrye
(But one step short of immortalitye)
Knowes more, thinks less, yet in a modest way
Concludes her yongest son hath in the play
Spoke sence to some mens wonder. If there be
In this strange age impossibilitye
The pen lookes to be canoniz'd that wrought
This miracle vpon yor eye & thought.

[*Exit m^{r}*]

3492 [*Exit m^{r}*]] heavily smudged out; reading uncertain